YOUR recipe could appear in our next cookbook!

Share your tried & true family favorites with us instantly at

www.gooseberrypatch.com

If you'd rather jot 'em down by hand, just mail this form to...
Gooseberry Patch • Cookbooks – Call for Recipes
PO Box 812 • Columbus, OH 43216-0812

If your recipe is selected for a book, you'll receive a FREE copy!

Please share only your original recipes or those that you have made your own over the years.

Recipe Name:

Number of Servings:

Any fond memories about this recipe? Special touches you like to add
or handy shortcuts?

Ingredients (include specific measurements):

D1611559

Instructions (continue on back if needed):

Special Code: **cookbookspage**

Over ➚

Extra space for recipe if needed:

Tell us about yourself...

Your complete contact information is needed so that we can send you your FREE cookbook, if your recipe is published. Phone numbers and email addresses are kept private and will only be used if we have questions about your recipe.

Name:

Address:

City: State: Zip:

Email:

Daytime Phone:

Thank you! Vickie & JoAnn

Fall
·FAMILY·
RECIPES

Gooseberry Patch

An imprint of Globe Pequot
246 Goose Lane
Guilford, CT 06437

www.gooseberrypatch.com
1•800•854•6673

Copyright 2018, Gooseberry Patch 978-1-62093-275-9

Do you have a tried & true recipe...

tip, craft or memory that you'd like to see featured in
a **Gooseberry Patch** cookbook? Visit our website at
www.gooseberrypatch.com and follow the
easy steps to submit your favorite family recipe.
Or send them to us at:

Gooseberry Patch
PO Box 812
Columbus, OH 43216-0812

Don't forget to include the number of servings your recipe makes,
plus your name, address, phone number and email address. If we
select your recipe, your name will appear right along with it...
and you'll receive a **FREE** copy of the book!

Contents

Dedication

Pumpkin spice and everything nice...that's what autumn days are made of!

Appreciation

A big thanks to everyone who shared their family's most treasured autumn recipes.

FARMHOUSE
Breakfasts

Apple Pancakes

June Sabatinos
Salt Lake City, UT

In the early 1980s, a friend served these delicious pancakes. She shared the recipe, and I have served them often since then. My family loves them served with apple syrup. It's a handy recipe since the batter can be made ahead of time. It also makes wonderful waffles... just add a little more flour to the batter.

1-3/4 c. milk	2 eggs, beaten
1/4 c. brown sugar, packed	2 c. all-purpose flour
1/4 c. oil	1 t. cinnamon
1-1/2 t. salt	1/4 t. nutmeg
1 env. active dry yeast	1 apple, peeled, cored
1/4 c. warm water, 110 to	and grated
115 degrees	

Heat milk just to boiling in a saucepan over medium heat. Stir in brown sugar, oil and salt until brown sugar dissolves. Set aside to cool slightly. In a large bowl, dissolve yeast in warm water; stir in eggs and milk mixture. In a separate bowl, mix together flour and spices; add to yeast mixture. Beat until smooth. Cover and let stand in a warm place for one hour, or until batter is light and bubbly. Fold in apple. Pour batter onto a greased hot griddle by 1/4 to 1/2 cupfuls. Cook until golden on one side; flip and cook on other side. May store batter in refrigerator up to 24 hours. Serves 6 to 8.

Spice up an autumn breakfast with cider-glazed sausages. Brown and drain 1/2 pound of breakfast sausage links. Add a cup of apple cider to the skillet, then turn the heat down to low and simmer for 10 minutes. Yum!

Light & Fluffy Waffles

Kathy Stewart
Elk Grove, CA

A handy recipe my grandma taught me. I love it because I can make the batter and then customize the waffle for each individual. Add fruit, nuts or chocolate chips to the batter for a variety of tastes. Banana and walnut waffles are fabulous!

2 eggs, separated
2 c. all-purpose flour
1-3/4 c. milk
1/2 c. oil
1 T. sugar

4 t. baking powder
1 T. ground flax seed
1 t. cinnamon
1/4 t. salt
1/2 t. vanilla extract

In a large bowl, combine egg yolks and remaining ingredients. Beat just until smooth; set aside. In a separate bowl, beat egg whites with an electric mixer on high speed until stiff peaks form. Fold egg whites into batter just until mixed. Grease a preheated waffle iron or spray with non-stick vegetable spray. Pour batter onto hot waffle iron by 1/2 cupfuls. Bake according to manufacturer's directions. Makes 6 waffles.

Make a scrumptious cinnamon apple topping. Sauté 3 cups sliced apples in a tablespoon of butter over medium-high heat until tender, about 8 minutes. Stir in 1/4 cup maple syrup and sprinkle with 1/2 teaspoon cinnamon. Serve warm.

Breakfast Egg Muffins

Joyceann Dreibelbis
Wooster, OH

School days, fun days...autumn is so busy! Make a large batch of these muffins and have a healthy to-go breakfast anytime. These tasty morsels can be wrapped and frozen, then just popped into the microwave for a quick hot breakfast.

1/2 c. mushrooms, diced
1 T. butter
7 eggs
2 c. shredded Cheddar cheese
1 c. cooked ham, bacon or
    sausage, diced
1/2 c. baby spinach, finely
    shredded

2 to 3 T. onion, chopped
2 T. green pepper, diced
2 T. red pepper, diced
salt and pepper to taste
Optional: grated Parmesan
    cheese

In a skillet over medium heat, sauté mushrooms in butter until tender; remove from heat and cool slightly. In a large bowl, beat eggs until smooth. Add mushrooms and remaining ingredients; mix well. Ladle egg mixture evenly into 12 greased muffin cups. Top with Parmesan cheese, if desired. Bake at 350 degrees for 25 minutes, or until set. Cool slightly before removing muffins from pan. Makes one dozen.

Take brunch outdoors! Spread out a quilt on the picnic table, gather everyone 'round and enjoy the colorful, sunny fall weather.

FARMHOUSE *Breakfasts*

French Toastwiches

Judy Lange
Imperial, PA

Kids love these banana-filled hot breakfast sandwiches...yum!

3 eggs, lightly beaten
1/3 c. milk
1 T. sugar
1/4 t. nutmeg
6 slices bread

1 to 2 T. butter, sliced
2 to 3 ripe bananas, sliced
Garnish: maple syrup, powdered
    sugar, honey or jelly

In a shallow bowl, combine eggs, milk, sugar and nutmeg; beat well. Dip each slice of bread into mixture until moistened on both sides. Melt butter on a griddle over medium heat. Add bread; cook until golden on both sides. To serve, arrange bananas over 3 French toast slices. Top with the remaining toast to make sandwiches. Serve hot, garnished as desired. Makes 3 sandwiches.

Bagel Sandwich

Vicki Lanzendorf
Madison, WI

My son came up with this one morning when I wouldn't take him to the fast-food restaurant that has them! They're quick to fix...the egg cooks while the bagel toasts. Using pre-cooked bacon or deli ham makes them super-fast and easy to eat on the run.

1 T. butter, divided
1 egg, beaten
1 to 2 T. milk
1 bagel, split and toasted

1 slice favorite cheese
2 slices pre-cooked bacon,
    warmed, or shaved deli ham,
    cut in half

Melt one teaspoon butter in a small skillet over low heat. Add egg and let cook through; do not stir or scramble. Meanwhile, spread remaining butter on toasted bagel. Top one bagel half with cheese and bacon or ham. Fold egg into quarters; place on top. Add remaining bagel half. Makes one sandwich.

All seasons sweet, but autumn best of all.
–Elinor Wylie

Bacon Breakfast Casserole

*Andrea Hickerson
Trenton, TN*

This is one of my most versatile recipes! It can be made up to a day ahead of time with just about any type of bread, breakfast meat and cheese you like. Simply refrigerate it until you're ready to bake.

6 slices white bread
1 lb. bacon, crisply cooked and
   crumbled
8 eggs, beaten
3 c. milk

1/4 t. salt
1/4 t. pepper
1/4 t. garlic powder
8-oz. pkg. shredded Cheddar
   cheese

Spray a 13"x9" baking pan with non-stick vegetable spray. Lay bread slices in the bottom of pan; spread bacon evenly over bread and set aside. In a large bowl, whisk together eggs, milk and seasonings; pour over bread. Spread cheese evenly over top. Bake, uncovered, at 350 degrees for 30 minutes, or until set. Cut into squares. Serves 8 to 10.

Small-town county fairs, food festivals, craft shows, swap meets...the list goes on & on. So grab a friend or two and go for good old-fashioned fall fun. A hearty warm breakfast will get you off to a terrific start.

Artichoke-Egg Squares

Deborah Patterson
Carmichael, CA

This is a very easy and delicious breakfast treat, perfect for any time of year. Serve some fresh fruit on a side and breakfast is ready.

8 eggs, lightly beaten
2 6-1/2 oz. jars artichoke
   hearts, drained and chopped
8-oz. pkg. shredded sharp
   Cheddar cheese

12 saltine crackers, crushed
1 onion, chopped
1 clove garlic, minced
salt and pepper to taste

In a large bowl, combine all ingredients and mix well. Pour into a greased 11"x8" baking pan. Bake, uncovered, at 325 degrees for 25 minutes, or until set. Cool slightly and cut into squares. Makes 6 servings.

The flimsy brown cardboard box with the red department store sticker was the first sign that a new school year was about to begin. New clothes, finally freed from layaway, being tried on to make sure that they fit properly. I was always excited to see what cute outfits Mom had picked out for me. One of my favorite clothing items was a black sweater dress decorated with purple circles and squiggles. I was definitely a child of the 80s! New book bags, lunchboxes, sneakers, even underwear! At school I got a new teacher, new pencils, new crayons and sometimes even new classmates. I had so many things to look forward to...walking to school with my friends, playing on the school playground, ice cream socials, school stores, scratch & sniff stickers on test papers, rainy fall days, and of course the childhood holy trinity of Halloween, Thanksgiving and Christmas. Such good memories!

–Nikisha House, Erie, PA

Baked Cinnamon-Apple French Toast Casserole

Bethi Hendrickson
Danville, PA

A wonderful addition to a family brunch or a retreat with friends. Wonderful with a cup of coffee, good company and lots of smiles.

1 c. brown sugar, packed
1/2 c. butter, melted
4 t. cinnamon, divided
1/2 t. allspice
4 apples, peeled, cored and
　　thinly sliced
3/4 c. sweetened dried
　　cranberries
1/2 c. chopped pecans, toasted
1 loaf French baguette, sliced
　　1/2-inch thick
6 eggs, beaten
1-1/2 c. milk
1 T. vanilla extract
1/4 t. nutmeg
Garnish: whipped cream

Combine brown sugar, butter, 2 teaspoons cinnamon and allspice in a large bowl; mix well. Add apples and toss to coat. Spread apple mixture evenly in a 13"x9" baking pan sprayed with non-stick vegetable spray. Sprinkle cranberries and pecans over apples. Arrange bread slices on top until completely covered; set aside. In a separate bowl, whisk together eggs, milk, vanilla, remaining cinnamon and nutmeg. Pour evenly over bread slices. Cover pan with aluminum foil and refrigerate for 6 to 24 hours. Bake at 375 degrees for 40 minutes. Remove foil; bake an additional 10 minutes, or until lightly golden. Let cool 5 minutes. Cut into squares; add a dollop of whipped cream. Serves 8 to 10.

Are breakfasts hurried at your house? Layer creamy yogurt, crunchy granola and juicy fresh berries in mini canning jars and tuck in the fridge. Perfect portions, ready to go!

FARMHOUSE *Breakfasts*

Easy Homemade Pancakes

*Wendy Jo Minotte
Duluth, MN*

*Why buy a mix when it's so easy to make your own from scratch?
We always make a big batch of pancakes because we love having
leftovers. It makes for a very easy breakfast the next day.*

4 eggs, beaten
1/2 c. canola oil
4 c. all-purpose flour
1 T. baking powder
3-1/2 c. milk

1/8 t. salt
4 T. plus 1 t. sugar
shortening for griddle
Garnish: butter, pancake syrup

In a large bowl, combine all ingredients except shortening and garnish;
beat until smooth. Grease a griddle with shortening; heat over medium
heat. Pour batter onto griddle by 1/4 cupfuls; cook until puffy and dry
around edges. Flip and cook other side until golden. Serve with butter
and syrup. Makes about 2-1/2 dozen small pancakes.

Mom's Scrumptious Apple Butter

*Lisa Ann Panzino DiNunzio
Vineland, NJ*

*My mom's homemade apple butter is a wonderful addition to
breakfast or brunch...but be aware that it will disappear quickly!*

14 Granny Smith apples, peeled,
   cored and quartered
1/2 c. dark brown sugar, packed
1/2 c. apple cider or apple juice

1 T. lemon juice
1 T. cinnamon
1/8 t. ground cloves

Add all ingredients to a 6-quart slow cooker; mix well. Cover and cook
on low setting for 8 hours. Uncover; mash apples. Cook, uncovered,
for 2 hours longer, stirring occasionally. Allow to cool. Transfer to an
airtight container; keep refrigerated. Makes about 3 cups.

Sunday Brunch Quiche

Amy Daily
Morrisville, PA

This is a wonderful dish. I used to make it on Sundays when my parents had brunch with my husband & me. It was a great way to get veggies into a dish without my dad picking them out! Since Dad has passed, I make it a lot more often, instead of just on special occasions. It has become one of my mom's favorite meals that I make for her...she always takes home the leftovers. I like to serve this with a fruit salad.

9-inch pie crust
3/4 lb. Italian pork sausage link,
    casing removed
2 T. butter
1 T. oil
8-oz. pkg. sliced mushrooms
1/2 sweet onion, diced
1 c. red pepper, diced

8-oz. pkg. shredded Colby-Jack
    cheese
5 eggs, beaten
3/4 c. half-and-half
1/2 t. dry mustard
1/4 t. salt
1/8 t. pepper

Press pie crust into a 9" pie plate; set aside. Brown sausage in a skillet over medium heat. Drain; transfer to a large bowl and set aside. Wipe out skillet with a paper towel. Add butter and oil to skillet. Add mushrooms; cover and sauté for 3 to 5 minutes. Add onion and red pepper; cook an additional 8 to 10 minutes. Add vegetables and cheese to sausage; mix well. Spoon into pie crust and set aside. In a separate bowl, whisk together remaining ingredients. Pour into pie crust to cover sausage mixture. Bake, uncovered, at 375 degrees for 40 to 45 minutes, until a knife tip inserted in the center tests clean. Let stand 5 minutes; cut into wedges. Makes 6 to 8 servings.

Add a savory crumb crust to your favorite quiche. Spread 2-1/2 tablespoons softened butter in a pie plate, then firmly press 2-1/2 cups buttery cracker crumbs into the butter. Freeze until firm, pour in filling and bake as directed.

FARMHOUSE *Breakfasts*

Orange Breakfast Knots

Renee Spec
Crescent, PA

*Tender, flavorful rolls...great with coffee for breakfast! I got this
recipe from a pre-school mom when I worked at a local school.*

1/4 c. warm water, 110 to
   115 degrees
1/4 c. warm milk, 110 to
   115 degrees
1 env. active dry yeast
1/4 c. plus 2 T. sugar, divided

1/2 t. salt
1 egg, beaten
1/4 c. butter, softened
2-1/2 c. all-purpose flour
1/4 c. butter, melted
zest of 1 orange

To a large bowl, add warm water and milk, yeast and 1/4 cup sugar;
stir until dissolved. Add salt, egg, softened butter and flour; blend well.
Cover and let stand for 30 minutes. Place melted butter, remaining
sugar and orange zest in 3 small bowls; set aside. Divide dough into
12 equal pieces; roll each piece into a 4-inch rope. Dip each into
butter, sugar and zest in bowls. Tie ropes into loose knots. Place knots
on a greased baking sheet; let rise in a warm place until double, about
45 minutes. Bake at 350 degrees for 15 to 20 minutes, until golden.
Makes one dozen.

Line a vintage tin lunchbox with a pretty tea towel
and fill with muffins or other baked goods...
perfect for a back-to-school buffet!

Fruit & Nut Granola Bars

Elizabeth McCord
Memphis, TN

Granola bars are a favorite snack for kids and adults alike. These delicious bars are packed full of good stuff...so easy to make at home that you'll never buy them at the store again!

1-3/4 c. quick-cooking oats, uncooked
3/4 c. crispy rice cereal
1/2 c. brown sugar, packed
1/3 c. all-purpose flour
1/2 t. salt
1/2 t. cinnamon
1/2 c. shredded coconut
1 c. chopped walnuts
3/4 c. slivered almonds
3/4 c. raisins

5-oz. pkg. sweetened dried cherries
5-oz. pkg. sweetened dried cranberries
1/2 c. mini semi-sweet chocolate chips
2/3 c. canola oil
1/3 c. creamy peanut butter
1/3 c. honey
1/4 c. hot water
2 t. vanilla extract

In a large bowl, combine oats, cereal, brown sugar, flour, salt, cinnamon and coconut; toss well. Add nuts, dried fruits and chocolate chips. Toss again; set aside. In a small bowl, mix together remaining ingredients; spoon over oat mixture and mix well. Divide between 2 greased 11"x7" baking pans; press down to flatten. Bake, uncovered, at 350 degrees for 20 to 22 minutes, until edges are golden. Let cool in pans. Cut into bars and store in an airtight container. Makes 16 bars.

Autumn is a good time to check your spice rack for freshness. Crush a pinch of each spice...if it has a fresh, zingy scent, it's still good. Toss out any old-smelling spices and stock up on ones you've used up during the year.

FARMHOUSE *Breakfasts*

Pumpkin Pie Oatmeal

Amanda Walton
Marysville, OH

A healthy breakfast that tastes just like everyone's favorite fall dessert! What could be better on a cool fall morning?

4 c. water
2 c. old-fashioned oats, uncooked
1/8 t. salt
1 c. canned pumpkin
1/2 c. brown sugar, packed

1 t. pumpkin pie spice
Optional: 1/2 c. chopped walnuts or pecans, 1/2 c. golden raisins
Garnish: milk or cream

Bring water to a boil in a medium saucepan over high heat. Stir in oats and salt; reduce heat to low. Simmer for about 10 minutes. Stir in pumpkin, brown sugar and spice; simmer another 5 minutes. Just before serving, stir in nuts or raisins, if desired. Serve warm with a splash of milk or cream. Serves 4.

Pecan Pie Muffins

Andrea Hickerson
Trenton, TN

A recipe shared with me by my sister. These are so easy and are simply decadent!

2 c. self-rising flour
2 c. brown sugar, packed
2 eggs, beaten

1 c. butter, melted and cooled slightly
1 c. chopped pecans

In a large bowl, combine all ingredients; mix well. Spoon batter into 12 paper-lined muffin cups, filling 1/2 full. Bake at 350 degrees for 20 minutes, or until golden. Makes one dozen.

Set the breakfast table the night before...enjoy a relaxed breakfast in the morning!

Sky-High Vegetable Pie

Gloria Morris
British Columbia, Canada

*I like to make this dish for our ladies' Bible Class brunches that
we have three or four times a year. It's a real hit with the fresh
tomatoes. So quick and easy to make...delicious too!*

6-oz. pkg. savory herb
    stuffing mix
5 eggs, divided
1 c. shredded mozzarella cheese,
    divided
10-oz. pkg. frozen chopped
    spinach, thawed, well
    drained and divided

1 red pepper, sliced
1 onion, chopped
3 tomatoes, sliced

Prepare stuffing mix according to package directions. Lightly beat
one egg and stir into stuffing mixture. Press mixture into a greased
9" springform pan to form a crust. Sprinkle 1/2 cup cheese over crust;
top evenly with half of spinach and all of red pepper and onion. Spread
remaining cheese and spinach over top; set aside. Beat remaining eggs;
pour over all. Top with tomato slices. Bake, uncovered, at 400 degrees
for 40 minutes, or until top of pie is completely set. Cut into wedges.
Serves 4.

Doughnut kabobs...a fun idea for a brunch buffet! Slide bite-size
doughnuts onto wooden skewers and stand the skewers in
a tall vase for easy serving.

Mom's Heavenly Ham Hash

Sandy Coffey
Cincinnati, OH

One day, I wanted to use some leftover ham and just mixed it together with some other ingredients, making it up as I went. A huge applause from the family for making something different! Perfect for a quick brunch that warms the soul.

3 T. butter, divided
3 c. cooked ham, diced
2 c. cooked potatoes, diced
1/2 c. onion, diced
salt and pepper to taste

1/2 c. light cream or milk
4 to 5 eggs
4 to 5 slices bread, toasted
Garnish: shredded Cheddar
  cheese

Melt 2 tablespoons butter in a large skillet over medium heat. Add ham, potatoes and onion; season with salt and pepper. Cook until heated through and lightly golden. Stir in cream or milk until hot and well mixed; cover and remove from heat. In a separate skillet over medium heat, melt remaining butter. Crack eggs into skillet and fry over easy. To serve, place toast slices on 4 to 5 plates. Top each with a scoop of hash, one egg and desired amount of cheese. Serve immediately. Serves 4 to 5.

Make breakfast waffle sandwiches for a delicious change.
Tuck scrambled eggs, a browned sausage patty and a slice
of cheese between waffles...yum!

Multi-Grain Waffles

Jill Burton
Gooseberry Patch

A hearty waffle that gets the day off to a good start!

2 c. buttermilk
1/2 c. old-fashioned oats,
   uncooked
2/3 c. whole-wheat flour
2/3 c. all-purpose flour
1/4 c. toasted wheat germ
1-1/2 t. baking powder
1/2 t. baking soda

1/4 t. salt
1 t. cinnamon
2 eggs, lightly beaten
1/4 c. brown sugar, packed
1 T. canola oil
2 t. vanilla extract
Garnish: butter, maple syrup
   or fruit jam

In a bowl, combine buttermilk and oats; let stand for 15 minutes. In a separate bowl, whisk together flours, wheat germ, baking powder, baking soda, salt and cinnamon; set aside. Stir eggs, brown sugar, oil and vanilla into oat mixture; add to flour mixture. Stir just until moistened. Spoon batter by 1/2 to 2/3 cupfuls onto a greased hot waffle iron. Bake according to manufacturer's directions. Makes 8 waffles.

Fall is sweater weather...hang an old-fashioned peg rack inside the back door so everyone knows just where to find their favorite snuggly sweater!

FARMHOUSE *Breakfasts*

Apple-Applesauce Muffins

Andrea Heyart
Savannah, TX

I have wonderful memories of making these muffins with my husband as newlyweds. We'd spend Saturday mornings playing in the kitchen, then we'd eat these muffins all weekend long for breakfast, dessert and midnight snacks.

1-3/4 c. all-purpose flour
1/2 c. sugar
2 t. baking powder
1/4 t. salt
1 t. cinnamon
1/4 t. nutmeg

1 egg, beaten
3/4 c. milk
1/2 t. vanilla extract
1/4 c. applesauce
3/4 c. apple, peeled, cored
   and diced

Combine flour, sugar, baking powder, salt and spices in a large bowl; toss together. Add egg, milk, vanilla and applesauce; stir to combine. Fold in apple. Spoon batter into 12 lightly greased or paper-lined muffin cups, filling 2/3 full. Bake at 400 degrees for 16 to 20 minutes, until tops are golden. Makes one dozen.

A baker's secret! Grease muffin cups on the bottoms and just halfway up the sides. Muffins will bake up nicely rounded on top.

Country Brunch Medley

Janis Parr
Ontario, Canada

I have tried many brunch dishes, but this one is so tasty and satisfying that it's the only one I make now. Sometimes I even make this delicious dish for supper. Since it's prepared a day in advance, it's perfect for potlucks and luncheons. Depending on your preferences, you may add whatever vegetables you like.

4 c. bread, cubed
8-oz. pkg. shredded Cheddar
　cheese
8 to 10 slices bacon, crisply
　cooked and coarsely chopped
1/2 c. mushrooms, chopped
1 c. tomatoes, chopped
1/3 c. white onion, chopped

1 c. cooked ham, cubed
10 eggs, well beaten
4 c. milk
1 t. dry mustard
1/4 t. onion powder
1 t. salt
1/4 t. pepper

The day before serving, spread bread cubes in the bottom of a greased deep 13"x9" baking pan. Sprinkle cheese over top. Layer with bacon, vegetables and ham; set aside. In a large bowl, beat together remaining ingredients. Carefully pour egg mixture over layered mixture in pan; do not stir. Cover and refrigerate for 24 hours. Bake, uncovered, at 325 degrees for 50 to 60 minutes, until set in the center. Serve piping hot. Serves 10 to 12.

Invite a best friend over to share tea and muffins on a
Saturday morning...it's a terrific way for the two of you
to spend time catching up!

Thelma's Lemony Fruit Salad

Janet Sharp
Milford, OH

Years ago, I attended a church Ladies' Circle once a month. A good friend would bring this salad for us to enjoy after the meeting. Very easy and a great choice when entertaining.

30-oz. can fruit cocktail
20-oz. can pineapple tidbits
15-oz. can mandarin oranges,
   drained

3 T. lemon juice
3 ripe bananas, sliced
3.4-oz. pkg. instant lemon
   pudding mix

In a large bowl, combine fruit cocktail with juice, pineapple tidbits with juice and mandarin oranges; set aside. In a separate bowl, drizzle lemon juice over banana slices to coat; add bananas to fruit mixture. Sprinkle dry pudding mix over all; stir gently to combine. Cover and chill at least 2 hours before serving. Serves 8 to 10.

Back-to-school time isn't just for kids. Treat yourself to a craft class like crocheting, jewelry making or scrapbooking that you've been longing to try...take a friend along with you!

Pull-Apart Apple-Nut Ring

Sue Klapper
Muskego, WI

With the convenience of refrigerated biscuits, you can have
this coffee cake ready to serve in a jiffy!

1/4 c. butter, melted
2/3 c. sugar
1 T. cinnamon
2 7-1/2 oz. tubes refrigerated
   buttermilk biscuits,
   separated

2 Granny Smith apples, peeled,
   cored, sliced and halved
   crosswise
1/3 c. nuts, chopped

Place melted butter in a bowl; set aside. Combine sugar and cinnamon
in a microwave-safe bowl. Microwave on high for 30 for 45 seconds,
until melted. Dip biscuits in butter; roll in sugar mixture. Arrange
biscuits in a lightly greased 11"x7" baking pan. Place an apple slice
between each biscuit and around outer edge of pan. Mix nuts with any
remaining sugar mixture; sprinkle over apples. Bake, uncovered, at
400 degrees for 25 to 30 minutes, until biscuits are deeply golden.
Serve warm. Makes 10 servings.

A delicious way to perk up a bowl of oatmeal...stir in a tablespoon
or two of canned pumpkin. Top with a sprinkle of pumpkin pie
spice. Good and good-for-you!

FARMHOUSE *Breakfasts*

Simple Sausage Pie

Tasha Petenzi
Goodlettsville, TN

This is a really easy breakfast dish that the whole family enjoys.
I like to make blueberry muffins to go along with it.

1 lb. ground hot pork sausage,
   browned and drained
1-1/2 c. shredded Cheddar or
   casserole-blend cheese

2 eggs, beaten
1 c. milk
1/2 c. biscuit baking mix

Spray a 9" pie plate with non-stick vegetable spray. Layer sausage and cheese in plate; set aside. In a bowl, whisk together eggs, milk and baking mix. Pour evenly over sausage and cheese. Bake, uncovered, at 400 degrees for 20 minutes, or until eggs are set and cheese is melted. Cut into wedges. Serves 6.

Barbara's Light Pancakes

Barbara Cebula
Chicopee, MA

When we want a fast breakfast with pancakes, these hit the spot.

2 eggs, beaten
2 c. milk
2 T. margarine, melted
2 c. all-purpose flour

2 t. baking powder
4 t. sugar
Garnish: warm maple syrup

Whisk eggs with milk and margarine in a large bowl. Add flour, baking powder and sugar; stir until batter is creamy with just a few lumps. Add batter by 1/4 cupfuls to an oiled hot skillet. Cook, turning once, until golden and cooked through. Serve immediately with warm maple syrup. Serves 4.

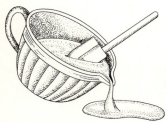

Mix pancake or waffle batter in a wide-mouth, spouted pitcher, then pour right onto the griddle...fewer dishes to wash!

Blueberry Cream Cheese Rolls

Donna Brandt
Churubusco, IN

When my youngest son comes home with his family, he usually wants these for breakfast at some time. The other kids want them all the time, but especially on holidays before the big meal.

1/4 c. warm water, 110 to
  115 degrees
2 T. plus 1 t. sugar, divided
1 env. active dry yeast
2 T. butter, softened
1-1/4 c. plus 2 T. milk, divided
1 egg, beaten

4 c. all-purpose flour
10-oz. jar blueberry preserves
1 c. fresh blueberries, or more
  if desired
2 c. powdered sugar
1/2 c. cream cheese, softened

In a small bowl, combine warm water, one teaspoon sugar and yeast. Let stand for 5 minutes. Meanwhile, in a separate large bowl, beat butter and remaining sugar with an electric mixer on medium speed until fluffy. Beat in 1-1/4 cups milk, egg and yeast mixture. Beat in flour on low speed. Transfer dough to a floured surface; knead for 2 minutes. Place in a greased bowl; cover and refrigerate overnight. In the morning, roll out dough 1/4-inch thick on a floured surface; spread with preserves and top with berries. Roll up dough, starting on one long edge; cut into 12 slices. Arrange slices in a 13"x9" baking pan sprayed with non-stick vegetable spray. Bake at 400 degrees for 20 to 25 minutes. For frosting, stir together powdered sugar, cream cheese and remaining milk until smooth. Frost rolls when slightly cooled. Makes one dozen.

Whip up a crock of maple butter to serve with freshly baked muffins or scones. Just combine 1/2 cup softened butter with 3/4 cup maple syrup and beat until fluffy...yum!

Jack-o'-Latte Coffee

Audrey Lett
Newark, DE

*We love our pumpkin spice coffee...now we can enjoy it
without going out for it!*

5 c. strong brewed coffee
4 c. milk
1/2 c. whipping cream
1/3 c. sugar
1/4 c. canned pumpkin

1 t. vanilla extract
1 t. pumpkin pie spice
Garnish: whipped cream,
    additional pumpkin pie spice

In a 3-quart slow cooker, combine all ingredients except garnish. Whisk until well combined. Cover and cook on high setting for 2 hours, stirring once after one hour. Serve in mugs, topped with a dollop of whipped cream and a sprinkle of spice. Makes 6 generous servings.

In October, on the Saturday before Halloween each fall,
our family gets together for our annual pumpkin carving party.
All the grandparents, aunts, uncles, cousins and friends gather to
carve pumpkins, eat chili, play games and spend a great time
together! Everyone brings a pumpkin to carve and a covered dish
to share. We give prizes for the best costume and the most creative
pumpkin. There's always a checkers competition, some crafts to do,
lots of laughs and a million pictures taken. It is a tradition I hope
we can continue for generations to come!
–Monica Britt, Fairdale, WV

Spinach & Feta Strata

Sandra Mirando
Depew, NY

Every year, I host a brunch celebrating all my friends' birthdays at one time, and this is a favorite. Great when you are having guests for brunch, since it is assembled the night before. Substitute Monterey Jack cheese if you prefer a milder taste, but the Pepper Jack cheese does not add too much spiciness to the strata.

6 croissants, cut in half
    horizontally
6 eggs, beaten
1-1/2 c. milk
1/2 t. salt
1/4 t. pepper
1/4 t. nutmeg

10-oz. pkg frozen spinach,
    thawed and drained
1-1/2 c. shredded Pepper Jack
    cheese
6-oz. container crumbled feta
    cheese

Arrange croissant halves with sides overlapping in a greased 13"x9" baking pan; set aside. In a bowl, whisk together eggs, milk and seasonings; stir in spinach. Pour mixture over croissants. Sprinkle cheeses over spinach mixture. Cover and refrigerate overnight. Uncover and bake at 350 degrees for 40 to 45 minutes, until lightly golden. Cut into squares and serve warm. Makes 6 to 8 servings.

When you rise in the morning, form a resolution
to make the day a happy one for a fellow creature.
–Sydney Smith

FARMHOUSE *Breakfasts*

Baked Eggs in Tomatoes

Gladys Kielar
Whitehouse, OH

A lovely breakfast presentation that's just a little different.

4 ripe beefsteak tomatoes
4 eggs
1/4 c. shredded Parmesan
   cheese

2 T. fresh oregano, chopped
1 clove garlic, halved
4 slices country-style bread
2 T. olive oil

Cut a slice off the top of each tomato; scoop out seeds and pulp. Arrange tomatoes cut-side up in a greased 8"x8" baking pan. Break an egg into each tomato; sprinkle with cheese and oregano. Bake, uncovered, at 425 degrees for 20 minutes, or until eggs are set with runny yolks. Rub garlic clove over bread slices and place on a baking sheet; drizzle with olive oil. Bake at 425 degrees for 6 minutes, or until toasted and golden. Place each filled tomato on a slice of toast and serve immediately. Serves 4.

Tyce's Terrific Taters

Tyce Smith
Valparaiso, IN

A mix-up created this terrific recipe when I was helping my mom cook breakfast for dinner!

6 T. butter
4 Yukon Gold potatoes,
   cubed

1-1/2 t. onion powder,
   or to taste
salt and pepper to taste

Melt butter in a skillet over medium-high heat. Add potatoes; cook for 5 minutes. Sprinkle with seasonings. Reduce heat to medium. Cover and cook, stirring occasionally, for 10 to 15 minutes, until tender and golden. Serves 4.

Add whimsy to your breakfast table with vintage salt & pepper shakers in fun shapes.

Fall Harvest Muffins

Normand Racette
Plymouth, NH

Just right for breakfast or even for a soup supper! These muffins freeze well. Remove from freezer a few hours before serving... warm slightly, if desired.

1-1/2 c. all-purpose flour
1-1/2 c. old-fashioned oats, uncooked
1 c. sugar
2 t. baking soda
1/2 t. salt
1 T. cinnamon
2 c. apples, cored and diced
1-1/2 c. carrots, peeled and shredded

3/4 c. sweetened dried cherries, coarsely chopped
1/2 c. chopped walnuts or pecans
3 eggs, beaten
1/2 c. butter, melted and cooled slightly
1/2 c. applesauce
2 t. vanilla extract

Combine flour, oats, sugar, baking soda, salt and cinnamon in a large bowl. Add apples, carrots, cherries and nuts; stir until well mixed. In a separate bowl, whisk together remaining ingredients. Add egg mixture to flour mixture; stir until just moistened. Spoon batter evenly into 18 greased or paper-lined muffin cups, filling 2/3 full. Bake at 350 degrees for 18 to 25 minutes, until a toothpick inserted in the center comes out clean. Cool 5 minutes; remove from pan. Serve warm or at room temperature. Makes 1-1/2 dozen.

Host a casual outdoor breakfast for family & friends... perfect for a sunny game day! Toss stadium blankets over tables and serve baskets of warm muffins, fresh fruit, homemade jams and creamy butter.

Strawberry-Glazed Fruit Salad

Becky Kuchenbecker
Ravenna, OH

A great refreshing salad to take to picnics or potlucks.

1 qt. fresh strawberries, hulled
   and halved
20-oz. can pineapple chunks,
   drained

4 firm bananas, sliced
16-oz. jar strawberry glaze

In a large bowl, gently toss together strawberries, pineapple and bananas; fold in glaze. Cover and chill for one hour before serving. Serves 4.

One of my favorite memories is of my mom making apple butter in the fall from the apples on our two apple trees. She could peel the apple in one long peel, which we got to eat. She had a hand-cranked gadget we put the cooked apples in, and smooshed it through the bottom holes. And there is no describing that smell! Now that she's older, my mom doesn't make apple butter as she used to. I'm going to see if we can make some today so I can get her recipe, I just realized time may be short. Maybe she will have some homemade rolls to toast to go with fresh apple butter.

–Rhonda Shaw, Conway, AR

Best Banana Bread Ever

Laura Klecha
Southington, OH

This recipe always turns out perfect! I love to have a slice for breakfast with coffee, especially while sitting on my back porch watching the birds.

1 c. all-purpose flour
3/4 c. whole-wheat flour
1 t. baking powder
1 t. baking soda
1/2 t. salt
1/4 t. cinnamon
2 eggs, beaten

3 ripe bananas, mashed
1 c. brown sugar, packed
3/4 c. oil
1/2 c. vanilla yogurt
1 t. vanilla extract
Optional: whipped cream cheese

In a bowl, combine flours, baking powder, baking soda, salt and cinnamon. In a separate large bowl, combine eggs, bananas, brown sugar, oil, yogurt and vanilla; mix well. Add flour mixture to banana mixture; stir gently but do not overmix. Pour batter into a greased 9"x5" loaf pan. Bake at 350 degrees for 70 minutes; cool. Serve with cream cheese, if desired. Makes one loaf.

Stock up on homemade jams and jellies at farmers' markets... you can't have too many! Bake up a batch of apple butter muffins, spoon raspberry jam into thumbprint cookies, glaze baked chicken with peach preserves. You can even add a cute fabric topper to turn a jar of jam into a last-minute hostess gift.

HOMETOWN
Get-Togethers

Cheese Party Pumpkin

Louise Graybiel
Ontario, Canada

Such a cute fall party appetizer! The rest of the year, just roll the ball in chopped parsley or nuts instead of decorating it with peppers.

8-oz. container sharp Cheddar
    cheese spread, room
    temperature
8-oz. pkg. light cream cheese,
    room temperature

1 t. garlic, finely chopped
1/8 t. hot pepper sauce
Garnish: green and yellow
    peppers
snack crackers or bread slices

With an electric mixer or a food processor, combine cheeses, garlic and hot sauce until blended well. Shape into a slightly flattened ball. Wrap in plastic wrap. Chill for at least 60 minutes to allow flavors to blend. At serving time, unwrap ball and place on a serving plate. With the tines of a fork or a small knife, draw vertical lines from the top of the ball to the bottom at evenly spaced intervals. Cut a "stem" from the green pepper and some triangles of yellow pepper to create a Jack-o'-Lantern face. Serve with crackers or bread. Serves 8.

Shake up your pumpkin display! Winter squashes come in many sizes, shapes and colors...they're as easy to carve as pumpkins. Green kabocha, bumpy gray Hubbard squash and mini sweet dumplings all make fun Jack-o'-Lanterns.

Autumn Caramel Apple Dip

Jackie Smulski
Lyons, IL

This fall dip makes a festive and tasty presentation when apples are in season...your family & friends will love it. It brings back memories of eating a caramel apple on a stick!

1-1/2 c. whipped cream cheese
1-1/4 c. caramel apple dip
8-oz. pkg. milk chocolate toffee
   baking bits

2 green apples, cored and sliced
   into wedges
2 red apples, cored and sliced
   into wedges

Spread cream cheese on a serving platter, leaving rim uncovered. Layer with caramel apple dip; sprinkle top with toffee bits. Arrange apple wedges on outer rim of platter, to form a circle. Serve immediately. Serves 8.

For no-stress entertaining, host an all-appetizers party! Set up tables in different areas so guests can mingle as they enjoy yummy spreads and finger foods. Your get-together is sure to be a scrumptious success.

Debbie's Walking Taco for a Crowd

*Debbie Muer
Encino, CA*

It's called a walking taco because you can take it anywhere! Great to snack on any time of the year, whether it's watching football games on TV in the fall or sitting by the pool in the summer. Great for taking to potlucks too.

4 16-oz. cans vegetarian refried beans
2 avocados, halved, pitted and mashed
16-oz. container sour cream
1-1/4 oz. pkg. taco seasoning mix
4-1/4 oz. can chopped black olives, drained

8-oz. pkg. shredded Cheddar cheese
8-oz. pkg. shredded Monterey Jack cheese
Garnish: chopped tomatoes and green onions
corn chips or nacho tortilla chips

In a clear glass bowl, layer refried beans and mashed avocados; set aside. Stir together sour cream and taco seasoning; spread over avocados. Continue layering with olives, cheeses, tomatoes and onions. Cover and chill until serving time. Serve with corn chips or tortilla chips. Serves 8 to 10.

Indian Summer is perfect for a neighborhood block party... the weather is still warm and fall foliage is gorgeous. Set up tables with hay bales to sit on. Everyone can snack on favorite finger foods while waiting for burgers and hot dogs to grill. Don't forget a game of beanbag toss for kids of all ages!

Bean Bowl Dip

Jessica Timberlake
Albany, OR

A simple, tasty, healthy snack that will please any crowd.
It has always been a big hit on game day!

15-1/2 oz. can black beans,
   drained and rinsed
1/2 c. fresh cilantro, chopped
1/2 c. tomato, chopped
1/2 c. onion, chopped
juice of 1/2 lemon

juice of 1/2 lime
1-1/4 oz. pkg. taco seasoning
   mix
salt and pepper to taste
tortilla chips

Add all ingredients except salt, pepper and chips to a blender or food processor. Blend on pulse to a creamy consistency. Transfer to a serving bowl; season with salt and pepper. Cover and chill until serving time. Serve with tortilla chips. Serves 6.

I was raised in a small town, but my dad, being a former police officer, never allowed me to trick-or-treat alone on Halloween. He also knew it was embarrassing for me to have my dad standing behind me as I went to each house, so he followed closely in the family car. We chose one of the more populated streets in town and would go up one side as far as my aunt's house, then back down the other side. Since my costumes always included a mask, my aunt wouldn't know who I was. I would ring her doorbell, call out "Trick-or-treat!" and wait for my candy. Afterwards, I would call her by name and thank her. Since she always had something special for the nieces & nephews, I usually ended up with an extra treat from her house. I will never forget those days, or the fact that Dad gave me the freedom to feel very grown-up while still being only a few feet away if I needed him.

–Lynn Grundstrom, Kennedy, NY

Sweet Potato Dip

Mel Chencharick
Julian, PA

I love sweet potatoes, so this recipe is one of my favorites.
This is different from most dips...really worth making!

2 to 3 sweet potatoes, peeled
   and quartered
2 T. pure maple syrup
1 T. butter, melted
1 T. lemon juice
1/2 t. ground ginger

1/8 t. nutmeg
1/8 t. pepper
Optional: 1/4 cup finely
   chopped pecans
assorted crackers

Cover sweet potatoes with water in a saucepan. Cook over medium-high heat until tender; drain and mash. Combine all ingredients except crackers; mix well. Serve warm or chilled with crackers. Serves 18.

Parsley-Walnut Pesto

Jill Ball
Highland, UT

This is a yummy dip. I serve it over chicken, mixed into pasta or as a spread for bread. It freezes well, so I will make up a huge batch and keep it for later. Great to have on hand for the holidays.

2 c. fresh parsley, coarsely
   chopped
3/4 c. chopped walnuts, toasted
1/2 c. grated Parmesan cheese
2 cloves garlic, pressed

1/2 t. salt
1 c. olive oil
2 T. lemon juice
2 t. lemon zest

Place parsley, walnuts, cheese, garlic and salt in a food processor. Pulse until well mixed; set aside. Combine oil, lemon juice, and zest in a small bowl. Add oil mixture to parsley mixture; pulse to combine. Serve immediately. To freeze, divide into small plastic freezer containers; cover and force out excess air. Freeze up to 3 months. Makes 12 servings.

Let guests know where the party is! Hang a
team banner on the porch.

Ranch Dressing Cheese Balls

Leona Krivda
Belle Vernon, PA

I make these often. They freeze well, so when you have guests drop in, it's nice to pull one out, let it thaw and serve. My children liked me having them in the freezer because whenever they were invited over by friends, they always grabbed one to take along.

1/2 c. mayonnaise
1/2 c. milk
1-oz. pkg. ranch salad
   dressing mix
1-1/2 c. cream cheese, softened

16-oz. pkg. finely shredded
   Cheddar cheese
5-oz. pkg. sliced almonds,
   toasted
snack crackers

Combine mayonnaise, milk and dressing mix in a stand mixer bowl; beat very well. Blend in cream cheese; add Cheddar cheese and mix well. Cover with plastic wrap; freeze for 30 to 40 minutes. Shape mixture into 2 balls; roll in almonds to coat. To freeze, wrap each ball in plastic wrap; place in plastic freezer bags and freeze. Thaw to serve. Serve with crackers. Makes 2 balls, one cup each.

Greet friends and neighbors with a harvest welcome! Set pumpkins on top of terra-cotta flower pots and line them up the front porch steps. So cheerful and so easy to do.

Cheese & Beef Dip in a Bread Bowl

Patti Harris
Hendersonville, TN

After discovering this yummy appetizer at a teacher luncheon, I've shared it with family at a number of get-togethers. Always a welcome treat!

1 round loaf French, Italian or
  Hawaiian bread
2 8-oz. pkgs. cream cheese,
  softened
16-oz. container sour cream
1.35-oz. pkg. onion soup mix,
  or less to taste

4-oz. pkg. sliced pressed beef
  or ham, chopped
1/2 c. celery, chopped
1/2 c. black olives, chopped

Cut off top of bread loaf. Tear top into chunks; pull chunks out of inside of bread to create a bowl effect. If desired, toast chunks in the oven to make dipping easier. Cover and set aside. In a bowl, mix together remaining ingredients. Dip may appear thin at first, but will set up. Spoon mixture into bread bowl. Cover and chill for at least one hour to allow flavors to blend and the dip to set. Serve with bread chunks. Serves 20.

Good Neighbor Day is always the fourth Sunday in September. The fall weather is ideal, so make it a day to visit and chat with neighbors, then enjoy a neighborhood potluck outdoors.

Smoked Turkey Dip with Pecans & Cherries

Tina Goodpasture
Meadowview, VA

I have always liked to cook. I also like to watch people enjoy what I fix. My Granny Hudson was the same way. She would always have a table full of food ready anytime of the day. You'd better come hungry, because you didn't leave her house until you ate something! Cream cheese, cherries and pecans...what else could you want?

8-oz. pkg. cream cheese, room
   temperature
1/4 c. mayonnaise
1 T. raspberry vinegar
1 c. deli smoked turkey, coarsely
   chopped
1/2 c. chopped pecans, toasted

1/4 c. dried tart cherries,
   finely chopped
pepper to taste
Garnish: pecan halves, whole
   dried cherries
crackers or sourdough bread

Combine cream cheese, mayonnaise and raspberry vinegar in a food processor; blend until smooth. Add turkey and process, pulsing, until a chunky paste forms. Transfer to a bowl; season with pepper. Stir in pecans and cherries. Spoon into a serving bowl. Cover and refrigerate up to 24 hours to allow flavors to blend. Let stand at room temperature 30 minutes before serving. Garnish with additional pecans and cherries. Serve with crackers or chunks of sourdough bread. Makes about 2-1/4 cups.

Make the sweetest harvest of "acorns" in a jiffy! With a dab of frosting, attach a mini vanilla wafer to a milk chocolate drop. Add a "stem" made from a bit of pretzel. Fill a bowl for nibbling, or top each dinner plate with 3 or 4 acorns.

Carilee's Perfect Buttermilk Ranch Dip

Crystal Branstrom
Russell, PA

I searched over 30 years for the perfect ranch dip recipe until my daughter brought this one home. It quickly became a treasured recipe of my family and many of our friends!

30-oz. jar mayonnaise
1-1/2 c. buttermilk
4 t. dried parsley

2 t. dried minced garlic
2 t. powdered flavor enhancer
1-1/2 t. garlic salt

Combine all ingredients in a large bowl. Whisk together until well blended. Cover and refrigerate until serving time. Serves 12.

Make a batch of warm crostini to serve with dips and spreads.
Thinly slice a loaf of French bread. Melt together 1/2 cup butter
with 1/2 cup olive oil and brush over one side of each slice.
Place on a baking sheet and bake at 300 degrees for a
few minutes, just until crisp and toasty.

S'Mores Dip

Jessalyn Wantland
Napoleon, OH

So good! Serve with chocolate graham crackers...yum!

2 8-oz. pkgs. cream cheese,
   softened
1 c. butter
1-1/2 t. vanilla extract
1-1/2 c. powdered sugar
1/4 c. brown sugar

6-oz. pkg. semi-sweet chocolate
   chips
Optional: 1-1/2 c. chopped
   pecans
chocolate graham crackers

In a large bowl, combine cream cheese and butter. Beat with an electric mixer on medium speed until fluffy. Stir in vanilla, sugars and chocolate chips; cover and refrigerate about one hour. To serve, form into mounds on a serving plate. Top with pecans, if desired. Serve with chocolate graham crackers. Makes 6 to 8 servings.

Arrange brightly colored autumn leaves on a clear glass plate,
then top with another glass plate to hold them in place.
Fill with assorted cheeses, crackers and crisp apple slices.

Pumpkin Pie Dip

Robyn Stroh
Calera, AL

*I wanted something different to take to a friend's house one night
and found this recipe. It was a hit...so simple and delicious!
Serve with gingersnaps or vanilla wafers.*

7-oz. jar marshmallow creme
8-oz. pkg. regular or light cream
   cheese, room temperature
1/2 c. to 3/4 c. canned pumpkin

1 to 2 t. pumpkin pie spice,
   to taste
1 to 3 T. powdered sugar,
   to taste

Combine marshmallow creme, cream cheese and pumpkin in a large
bowl. Beat with an electric mixer on medium speed until well combined
and smooth. Add spice and powdered sugar in smallest amounts first;
stir together. Adjust to your taste. For best flavor, cover and refrigerate
overnight before serving. Serves 12 to 15.

Pecan-Cranberry Spread

Leona Krivda
Belle Vernon, PA

*This recipe is so easy to make, yet it is so good. I have
handed out the recipe many times.*

8-oz. pkg. cream cheese,
   softened
1/4 c. frozen orange juice
   concentrate, thawed

1/2 c. chopped pecans
1/2 c. sweetened dried
   cranberries, minced
assorted crackers

In a large bowl, beat cream cheese with an electric mixer on medium
speed until soft and fluffy. Add orange juice; mix well. Add pecans
and cranberries; blend in well. Cover and refrigerate until serving time.
Serve with crackers. Makes 2 cups.

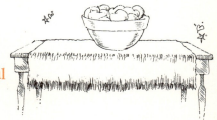

Lengths of burlap are so easy to
turn into a table runner...simply
cut and fringe the edges! Wonderful
for harvest-time gatherings.

Buffalo Cauliflower Bites

Liz Plotnick-Snay
Gooseberry Patch

We love buffalo chicken wings when we're watching football on television, but sometimes we want to lighten up a little. These crisp, spicy bites are just the thing!

1/2 c. all-purpose flour
1/2 c. milk
1 t. garlic powder
1/2 t. paprika
1/4 t. ground cumin
1/2 t. salt

1/4 t. pepper
1 head cauliflower, cut into large
   flowerets
2/3 c. hot wing sauce
2 T. butter, melted
Garnish: ranch salad dressing

In a large bowl, whisk together flour, milk and seasonings. Add cauliflower; toss to coat. Spread cauliflower evenly on a baking sheet coated with non-stick vegetable spray. Bake at 450 degrees for 15 minutes, turning once. Meanwhile, in another large bowl, stir together pepper sauce and melted butter. Add baked cauliflower; toss to coat and return to baking sheet. Bake for another 20 to 25 minutes, until crisp, turning once. Serve with ranch dressing. Serves 8 to 10.

Clear glass votives can be made into the prettiest fall mantel lights. Cut strips of tissue paper in fall colors and arrange on the outside of votive holders with découpage medium. Seal them to the glass with another coat of découpage medium, then let dry before tucking candles inside.

Soft & Sweet Onion Rings

Wendy Jo Minotte
Duluth, MN

These onion rings taste so good that they disappear as fast as I can make them! There are never any leftovers, and my family always wishes there were more. To drain them, I lay a clean brown paper bag over a large baking sheet and then put a layer of paper towels on top of that.

2 eggs, beaten
1 c. milk
1-1/2 c. all-purpose flour
1 t. salt

4 yellow onions, thinly sliced
   and separated into rings
oil for frying
salt to taste

In a shallow bowl, whisk together eggs, milk, flour and salt until smooth. Dip each onion ring into batter, allowing excess batter to drip into bowl. In a Dutch oven over medium-high heat, heat 2 inches of oil to about 365 degrees. Add several onion rings at a time; cook for about 2 minutes, turning once, until golden. Drain on paper towels; season with additional salt. Serve warm. Makes 6 to 8 servings.

Serve your favorite hot or cold dip spooned into crisp wonton cups...so easy, yet so impressive! Coat a muffin tin with non-stick vegetable spray, then press a wonton wrapper gently into each cup. Spritz with a little more of the spray and bake at 350 degrees for 8 minutes, or until golden. Fill as desired.

Fresh Veggies with Dill Dip

*Eu-Det Crawford
New Madison, OH*

*My mother-in-law has made this wonderful recipe for years.
It is one of the first things that we make when the vegetables
start coming in from the garden.*

1 c. sour cream
1 c. mayonnaise
1 T. Beau Monde seasoning
1 T. dried parsley
1 T. dill seed

sliced fresh vegetables such as
carrots, celery, cauliflower,
broccoli and green or red
peppers

Combine all ingredients except vegetables; mix well. Cover and
refrigerate for at least 2 hours. To serve, set the chilled dip in the center
of a large platter and arrange vegetables around the dip. Serves 8 to 10.

Bacon-Filled Cherry Tomatoes

*Cathy Foelske
DeKalb, IL*

*I make this for game days and special holidays. It is a favorite
of my husband's. I have been making it for 25 years.*

24 cherry tomatoes
1 lb. bacon, crisply cooked
and crumbled
1/2 c. mayonnaise
2 T. grated Parmesan cheese

1/2 c. green onion, finely
chopped
2 T. fresh parsley, chopped
Optional: additional bacon or
fresh parsley

Cut a thin slice off the top of each tomato. With a melon scoop,
carefully hollow out tomatoes, leaving a shell 1/8-inch thick. Set
tomatoes cut-side down on paper towels to drain. Meanwhile, combine
bacon, mayonnaise, cheese, onion and parsley; stir until well blended.
Spoon mixture into tomatoes. Cover and chill several hours to blend
flavors. Garnish as desired. Makes 2 dozen.

Hollow out some apples for
clever tea light holders.

Cheese-Stuffed Pea Pods

Janis Parr
Ontario, Canada

I got to enjoy these appetizers at our girls' night out potluck recently. They are so yummy with the creamy filling!

2 c. water
1/2 lb. sugar snap pea pods
8-oz. pkg. cream cheese,
   softened
1/2 c. shredded Cheddar cheese

1/8 t. salt
1/8 t. pepper
2 drops Worcestershire sauce
1 t. onion, finely minced

In a saucepan over medium-high heat, bring water to a full boil. Add pea pods. Boil for one full minute; drain well. Plunge pea pods into ice water for one minute; drain well. Trim stems and cut seam on the side of each pea pod, forming a pocket; set aside. In a bowl, combine cheeses, seasonings and Worcestershire sauce. With an electric mixer on medium speed, beat until well mixed. Stir in onion. Spoon or pipe cheese mixture into pocket of each pea pod. Cover and chill well. Makes about 4 dozen.

Stuffed Celery

Jamie Stallman
Cincinnati, IA

This is a staple at our family's Thanksgivings. It just wouldn't be right if we didn't have this on the table! It's a great snack to hold everyone over until the turkey is done.

2 8-oz. pkgs. cream cheese,
   softened
3/4 c. green olives with
   pimentos, diced

1 bunch celery, cut into 3-inch
   sticks

Blend cream cheese and olives. Spread mixture into celery sticks; Cover and chill until serving time. Makes about 24 servings.

Lighten up! Reduced-fat cream cheese is just as tasty in most recipes for dips and spreads.

Freeze-Ahead Crab Appetizers

Sharon Taylor
Bloomington, MN

These tasty bites will stay good in the freezer for six months...so handy for the holidays. They're quick & easy to make and oh-so good!

1/2 c. butter
5-oz. jar sharp pasteurized
   process cheese spread
1-1/2 t. mayonnaise

1/2 t. garlic salt
1/2 t. seasoned salt
7-oz. can crabmeat, drained
6 English muffins, split

In a large bowl, combine all ingredients except muffins; blend well. Spread mixture on cut sides of muffin halves. Arrange on baking sheets; freeze until solid. Remove from freezer; cut each muffin half into wedges. Place wedges in a plastic freezer bag; return to freezer. To serve, arrange frozen appetizers on a baking sheet. Broil for 10 to 12 minutes, until bubbly and golden. Serve hot. Makes about 4 dozen.

The secret to being a relaxed hostess...choose foods that can be prepared in advance. At party time, simply pull from the fridge and serve, or pop into a hot oven as needed.

Mexican Corn & Black Bean Dip
Maressa Smith
Wauneta, NE

This simple dip can be put together in ten minutes. I made it for a party and it was gone before all the other appetizers!

1/2 c. mayonnaise or mayonnaise-style salad dressing
1/2 c. sour cream
11-oz. can sweet corn & diced peppers, drained
15-1/2 oz. can black beans, drained

4-oz. can diced green chiles, drained
4-1/4 oz. can chopped black olives, drained
tortilla chips or snack crackers

In a bowl, combine all ingredients except tortilla chips or crackers; mix well. Cover and chill for about one hour. Serve with chips or snack crackers. Serves 12 to 15.

October is the ideal time to plant daffodils, tulips and other spring flowering bulbs! There are lots of varieties to choose from at the neighborhood garden center. Why not pick up a few extra bulbs to give as gifts?

HOMETOWN
Get-Togethers

Fiesta Pinwheels

Jennifer Tanner
Smithport, PA

These taste as festive as they look! This recipe is a must for our gatherings with family & friends. Make them the day before and slice just before the party. They won't last long!

2 8-oz. pkgs. cream cheese,
    softened
1-oz. pkg. fiesta ranch dip mix
4-oz. jar sliced pimentos,
    drained
4-oz. can diced green chiles,
    drained

2-1/4 oz. can chopped black
    olives, drained
2 green onions, minced
6 10-inch flour tortillas

In a large bowl, combine cream cheese and dip mix; blend well. Stir in remaining ingredients except tortillas; spread evenly over tortillas. Roll up tightly; place on a plate and cover. Chill for 2 hours or overnight. At serving time, cut into one-inch slices. Serves 10 to 12.

Party fun! Fill a big jar with pieces of candy corn...don't forget to count them first. Ask everyone to guess how many pieces are in the jar. Send the jar home with the person whose guess is the closest!

Game-Day Guacamole

Nancy Albers Shore
Cheyenne, WY

This is so quick & easy! Fresh cilantro makes all the difference.
By halftime, I usually have to make a second batch! Be sure to
select avocados that are ripe but not mushy.

3 ripe avocados, halved and
   pitted
2 roma tomatoes, seeded and
   diced
3 green onions, thinly sliced
1/4 c. fresh cilantro, chopped

1 to 2 T. lime juice
Optional: 1 jalapeño pepper,
   seeded and chopped
salt to taste
tortilla chips or crackers

Scoop out avocados into a bowl. With a fork, mash avocado until just
slightly chunky. Add remaining ingredients except salt and chips or
crackers; stir gently. Season with salt to taste. Serve with tortilla chips
or crackers. Serves 6.

When I was a young girl growing up on a Nebraska farm,
fall was my favorite time of year. I loved being outdoors after
school, traipsing around the farm with my cat and a good book.
I would find a spot in the pasture, put a blanket down and lie in
the tall grass to read in the waning sunshine, my cat by my side.
At dusk, I would gather up my blanket, book and cat and make
my way to the barn, where I knew my dad would be doing the
evening milking. I'd hang out in the barn, talking with Dad,
petting the cow and laughing at all the farm cats when he shot
milk from the cow's teat into their mouths. Walking back to the
house with Dad after milking, in the crisp, ever-growing darkness,
holding his hand always made me feel so loved and lucky to be
living on the farm. We would go into the warm, brightly lit house
to a tasty homemade dinner that Mom had made. I miss those
times and would go back to them in a heartbeat.

–Brenda Taylor, Lincoln, NE

Parmesan Cheese Puffs

Sherry Bateman
Fulton, NY

I always get asked for this recipe. I usually bring it to parties right on the baking sheet, so I can bake them at the gathering. The house smells great and they can be served warm, right out of the oven.

3/4 c. mayonnaise
1 c. grated Parmesan cheese

1 bunch green onions, sliced
6 English muffins, split

Combine mayonnaise, Parmesan cheese and onions in a bowl; blend well. Spread mixture on cut sides of muffins; place on a baking sheet. Watching very closely, broil for 5 minutes, or just until bubbly and golden. Cut muffin halves into quarters with kitchen shears; serve warm. Makes 4 dozen.

Artichoke Spread with Kalamata Olives

Kitra Ludlow
Bloomington, IN

Wonderful for family get-togethers...we love this!

2 c. mayonnaise
1-1/4 c. grated Parmesan
   cheese, divided
1 c. Kalamata olives, pitted
   and chopped

3 c. canned artichokes, drained
   and chopped
sliced French bread

Mix together all ingredients except bread, reserving 1/4 cup cheese for garnish. Spread in a lightly greased one-quart casserole dish. Sprinkle reserved cheese on top. Bake, uncovered, at 350 degrees for 20 to 25 minutes, until heated through and golden on top. Serve warm with sliced French bread. Serves 6 to 8.

Fill up a big party tray with colorful crisp veggies for dipping. Calorie-counting friends will thank you!

Candy Apple Snack Crunch

Megan Brooks
Antioch, TN

Autumn has lots of occasions for crunchy snacking...back to school,
tailgate parties, Halloween and Thanksgiving get-togethers.
Mix up a big batch of this yummy snack that's sure to be a hit!

3 c. bite-size crispy corn cereal
    squares
3 c. bite-size crispy rice cereal
    squares
3 c. bite-size crispy wheat cereal
    squares
1 c. pecan halves

1/4 c. butter
1/4 c. water
1/4 c. sugar
1/2 c. red cinnamon candies
1 c. dried apple pieces, coarsely
    chopped
cinnamon to taste

Mix cereals and pecans in an ungreased roasting pan; set aside. In a
heavy large saucepan, combine butter, water, sugar and candies. Cook
and stir over medium heat until sugar is dissolved and candies are
melted. Pour over cereal mixture; stir until evenly coated. Spread in
roasting pan. Bake, uncovered, at 300 degrees for 20 minutes. Stir in
apples; bake for 15 minutes longer. Spread on wax paper-lined baking
sheets and cool, about 20 minutes. Sprinkle with cinnamon. Store in
an airtight container. Makes 11 cups.

For a Halloween party, offer a selection of creepy foods
and beverages...label with table tents in your spookiest
handwriting. Have a specialty that isn't Halloween-ish?
Just give it a spooky new name!

HOMETOWN
Get-Togethers

Pumpkin Seeds & Cherries Snack Mix

Lori Rosenberg
University Heights, OH

Always a fan favorite, especially for those who still try to eat healthy on game day!

2 c. pumpkin seeds
3/4 c. sunflower seeds
1 c. slivered almonds

6 T. pure maple syrup
coarse salt to taste
1 c. dried cherries or cranberries

In a large bowl, combine pumpkin seeds, sunflower seeds and almonds; toss to mix. Drizzle with syrup and stir until evenly coated. Divide mixture between 2 parchment paper-lined baking sheets, spreading evenly. Season with salt. Bake at 300 degrees for about 20 minutes, stirring several times with a wooden spoon, just until golden. Cool mixture completely on baking sheets. Add cherries and toss to combine. Store in an airtight container at room temperature. Makes 6 cups.

Cool-weather fun makes everyone hungry, so take along some treats for munching. Pick up some new paper paint pails from the hardware store to decorate with cut-outs and paint. Fill with snack mix or popcorn and wrap up in clear cellophane...yum!

Maple Snack Mix

Judy Swoboda
College Station, TX

When my friend from Vermont sent me a big jug of maple syrup, I was all set to make some goodies! I found this basic recipe in a magazine and made a few personal touches to it. It's always a big hit at gatherings with family & friends.

2 c. bite-size crispy corn cereal
    cereal squares
2 c. bite-size crispy rice cereal
    cereal squares
2 c. doughnut-shaped honey nut
    oat cereal

2 c. sesame sticks
1 c. chopped pecans
1/2 c. pure maple syrup
1-1/2 T. butter
1 t. vanilla extract
1 t. maple flavoring

In a large bowl, mix together cereals, sesame sticks and pecans. Pour into a 13"x9" baking pan coated with non-stick vegetable spray; set aside. Combine syrup and butter in a microwave-safe cup; microwave for 30 seconds. Add vanilla and maple flavoring to syrup mixture. Pour syrup mixture over cereal mixture; stir to coat well. Bake, uncovered, at 300 degrees for 45 minutes, stirring every 15 minutes. Store in an airtight container. Makes 10 cups.

Single servings! Fill paper muffin cups with crackers, snack mix and pretzels. Arrange on a tiered stand so guests can help themselves.

Seasoned Pumpkin Seeds

Laurel Perry
Loganville, GA

One of my favorite parts of Halloween is pumpkin carving. I love pumpkin seeds. This is a tasty twist on the usual roasted seeds.

3/4 c. pumpkin seeds, cleaned,
   rinsed and patted dry
1 T. butter, melted

1/2 t. Worcestershire sauce
1/4 t. garlic salt
1/4 t. seasoned salt

Place pumpkin seeds in a lightly greased 8"x8" baking pan. Add remaining ingredients; stir to thoroughly coat all sides. Bake, uncovered, at 300 degrees for 25 to 30 minutes, stirring occasionally, until lightly toasted. Makes 3/4 cup.

Smoky Roasted Pecans

Tina Wright
Atlanta, GA

Perfect for munching on a nature hike...welcome on any appetizer table.

1-1/2 c. pecan halves
2 T. pure maple syrup
2 t. olive oil

1 t. smoked sweet paprika
1/2 t. salt
1/8 t. cayenne pepper

Combine all ingredients in a bowl; mix well. Spread on a parchment paper-lined baking sheet. Bake at 400 degrees for 12 to 15 minutes, tossing halfway through, until golden. Cool before serving. Makes 1-1/2 cups.

October gave a party;
The leaves by hundreds came.
The chestnuts, oaks and maples,
And leaves of every name.

–George Cooper

Wild West Wings

Janis Parr
Ontario, Canada

This yummy, quick & easy recipe is perfect for casual parties.

20 chicken wings, separated
1/2 c. catsup
1/4 c. water
1/4 c. white vinegar
1/4 c. brown sugar, packed

2 T. honey
1 t. Dijon mustard
1 t. Worcestershire sauce
1/2 t. ground ginger
1 clove garlic, minced

Preheat a broiler pan in oven set to broil; arrange wings on pan. Broil for 5 to 7 minutes, until slightly crisp. Turn wings over; broil on other other side until golden. Meanwhile, combine remaining ingredients in a bowl; mix well. Turn oven to 375 degrees. Generously brush sauce over wings. Bake, uncovered, for 30 minutes, occasionally brushing with remaining sauce. Serve hot. Makes 40 pieces.

Make a tabletop Halloween tree for your party! Choose a branch from the backyard. Spray-paint it black, if you like, and stand it securely in a weighted vase. Wind with twinkling orange or purple lights...trim with spooky black crows, tiny ghosts made of white hankies and mini Jack-o'-Lanterns. Boo!

HOMETOWN
Get-Togethers

Chicken-Fried Bacon

Sherrie Loncon
Orange, TX

I came across this recipe while traveling many, many years ago in San Antonio, Texas. The taste is indescribably good!

2 eggs, beaten
1 c. milk
1 c. all-purpose flour
salt and pepper to taste

1 lb. bacon
1/2 c. shortening
Garnish: ranch salad dressing

Whisk together eggs and milk in a shallow bowl; set aside. Blend flour, salt and pepper in a separate bowl. Dip each slice of bacon into egg mixture; roll in seasoned flour. Melt shortening in a skillet over medium heat. Add bacon, a few slices at a time. Cook until crisp and golden; drain. Serve with ranch dressing. Serves 8 to 10.

Mini Honey-Mustard Chicken Bites

Jamie Comstock
Potlatch, ID

Football Sundays are a family affair around my house! I came up with this recipe when I needed a quick appetizer.

12-oz. tube refrigerated biscuits
1 c. cooked chicken, finely
  chopped
1/4 c. real bacon bits

1/4 c. shredded mozzarella
  cheese
1/4 c. honey-mustard salad
  dressing

Separate dough into 10 biscuits; cut each biscuit in half. Press into the bottom and up the sides of 20 ungreased mini muffin cups; set aside. Combine remaining ingredients. Spoon 2 teaspoons chicken mixture into each cup. Bake at 400 degrees for 8 to 10 minutes, until crust is golden. Remove from cups; serve warm. Makes 20.

Pizza Nachos

Kassie Frazier
West Point, TN

As a busy mom of three, I'm always looking for speedy dishes to make...time isn't something I have a lot of! This came to me one day, and it really is simple and delicious.

9-oz. pkg. tortilla chips
8-oz. pkg. shredded pizza-blend
  cheese
8-oz. pkg. sliced pepperoni
10 slices bacon, crisply cooked
  and crumbled

1 lb. ground pork sausage,
  browned and drained
Optional: 4-1/4 oz. jar chopped
  black olives, drained

Spread tortilla chips in an ungreased 13"x9" baking pan. Layer with remaining ingredients. Bake, uncovered, at 350 degrees for 10 minutes, or until cheese is melted. Serves 4 to 6.

Host a pumpkin painting party. Provide acrylic paints, brushes and plenty of pumpkins...invite kids to bring their imagination and an old shirt to wear as a smock. Parents are sure to join in too!

Cheesy Deviled Eggs

Joanna Nicoline-Haughey
Berwyn, PA

Tangy cheese and crispy bacon give these deviled eggs a twist on the traditional recipe. They might be your new favorite!

1 doz. eggs, hard-boiled and
   peeled
1/2 c. mayonnaise
5 slices bacon, crisply cooked
   and crumbled

2-1/2 T. finely shredded sharp
   Cheddar cheese
1 T. mustard

Slice eggs in half lengthwise. Scoop out egg yolks and place in a bowl. Arrange egg whites on a serving plate and set aside. Mash egg yolks with a fork. Add remaining ingredients; mix well. Spoon yolk mixture into whites. Cover and chill until serving time. Makes 2 dozen.

If you're making hard-boiled eggs, use eggs that have been refrigerated at least 7 to 10 days, instead of fresher eggs... the shells will slip right off.

Spiced Apple Cider

Rogene Rogers
Kalispell, MT

When we were first married, we lived in Connecticut. We loved going to a favorite apple orchard to pick apples on a crisp fall day and enjoy a cup of hot apple cider in their indoor market. Now, over 40 years and several moves across country later, we still have fond memories whenever we enjoy this...their original recipe! It is so easy to make and best part is that it has no added sugar.

2 qts. fresh apple cider
3 whole cloves

2 3-inch cinnamon sticks
Optional: lemon or orange slices

Combine cider and spices in a 3-quart slow cooker. Cover and cook on low setting for 2 to 3 hours. Remove spices with a slotted spoon. If desired, float a lemon or orange slice in each mug. Serves 8 to 10.

Pitch a tent in the backyard on a fall night so the kids can camp out, tell ghost stories and play flashlight tag.
What a great way to make memories!

Get-Togethers

Company's Coming Punch

Lisanne Miller
Wells, ME

This punch can be made a day ahead to allow the flavors to come together. Serve it ice-cold. We like to make ice cubes with cranberries in them for a festive look!

48-oz. bottle white cranberry-
  peach juice drink, chilled
2-ltr. bottle lemon-lime soda,
  chilled

2-ltr. bottle peach soda, chilled
1 orange, sliced
1 lime, sliced
ice cubes or ice ring

In a large pitcher, combine all ingredients except orange and lime slices. Cover and chill at least 8 hours. At serving time, pour into a punch bowl. Add orange and lime slices along with festive ice cubes or an ice ring. Serves 18 to 24.

For a fruit-studded ice ring that won't dilute your holiday punch, arrange sliced oranges, lemons and limes in a ring mold. Pour in a small amount of punch and freeze until set. Add enough punch to fill mold and freeze until solid. To turn out, dip mold carefully in warm water.

Aunt Jo's Red-Hot Punch

Ramona Wysong
Barlow, KY

This is a recipe that my Aunt Jo Hartman has made,
and it's really great for fall get-togethers.

8 c. water
9-oz. pkg. red cinnamon
   candies
5 4-inch cinnamon sticks
46-oz. can unsweetened
   pineapple juice

46-oz. can unsweetened
   apple juice
2 6-oz. cans frozen orange juice
   concentrate, thawed
6-oz. can frozen lemonade
   concentrate, thawed

In a large stockpot, combine water, candies and cinnamon sticks. Bring
to a boil over high heat; cook and stir until candies dissolve. Remove
cinnamon sticks; add remaining ingredients and mix well. Heat
through; serve hot. Makes about 45 small servings.

Bewitching Brew

Kendall Hale
Lynn, MA

Perfect for a Halloween party! So quick...just stir together and serve.

64-oz. bottle cranberry-grape
   juice drink, chilled
4 c. grape-flavored ginger ale,
   chilled

1 pt. raspberry sherbet

Pour juice into a large punch bowl. Carefully pour in ginger ale. Spoon
scoops of sherbet into punch. Makes 24 small servings.

A punch bowl makes even the
simplest party beverage special!
Surround it with a grapevine
wreath decorated with colorful
mini pumpkins and fall leaves.

Glazed Pecans

Kay Helbert
Castlewood, VA

These are a nice little treat to share with neighbors.

3 c. pecan halves
1/2 c. water
1 c. sugar
1/2 t. salt

3/4 t. cinnamon
1/4 t. nutmeg
1 t. rum flavoring or vanilla
extract

Spread pecans in a 15"x10" jelly-roll pan sprayed with non-stick vegetable spray. Bake at 250 degrees for 15 minutes, or until toasted; remove from oven. Meanwhile, combine water, sugar and spices in a heavy saucepan. Cook over medium-high heat until mixture reaches the soft-ball stage, or 234 to 243 degrees on a candy thermometer. Remove from heat. Add flavoring and toasted pecans. Stir until well coated. Pour onto wax paper and separate pecans as they cool. Makes 3 cups.

I have many treasured memories of autumn, my favorite season. One of my favorites is of a perfect fall day in 2010 that my mom & I spent together. Though we live in a city, we are blessed with a little patch of country, an apple orchard called Brooksby Farm. Every October, the local historical society holds a craft fair in the barn there. This day was the quintessential New England fall day...cool and crisp, bright sun against a brilliant blue sky, smoke curling out of chimneys, leaves swirling. Mom & I enjoyed the craft fair, then headed outside to the old-fashioned popcorn vendor for a treat. After that we went up the road a bit, past the pumpkin patch to the farm store for hot cider, doughnuts and coffee! Then, shopping at the craft store where we scooped up lots of autumn crafting goodies! And home with the memories of our perfect fall day together. I spent the rest of the afternoon with my husband and dog, enjoying that beautiful late-afternoon golden fall light.

–Kristen DeSimone, Peabody, MA

Marcie's Quick & Cheesy Cocktail Swirls

Leona Krivda
Belle Vernon, PA

My daughter Marcie hosted a party, and this is one of the appetizers that she served. They are very, very good!

3-oz. pkg. cream cheese, softened
5 slices bacon, crisply cooked and crumbled
2 T. onion, finely chopped
1 t. milk

8-oz. tube refrigerated crescent rolls
8-oz. jar pasteurized process cheese sauce, room temperature
grated Parmesan cheese to taste

In a large bowl, combine cream cheese, bacon, onion and milk; blend well and set aside. Separate crescent rolls into 4 rectangles; press perforations to seal. Spread a little cheese sauce on each rectangle; spread 1-1/2 tablespoons cream cheese mixture on each. Roll up, starting at the long edge; press to seal. Cut each roll into 8 pieces. Place pieces cut-side down on an ungreased baking sheet. Lightly sprinkle with Parmesan cheese. At this point, swirls may be refrigerated up to 2 hours before baking. Bake at 375 degrees for 12 to 15 minutes; serve warm. May also wrap in aluminum foil and freeze in a plastic freezer bag. To serve, thaw in foil; loosen foil and reheat at 350 degrees for 8 to 10 minutes. Makes 2-1/2 dozen.

Be sure to have some finger foods for the kids...
tortilla pinwheels, cheese cubes, apple wedges and
mini pigs-in-a-blanket are terrific for little tailgaters.

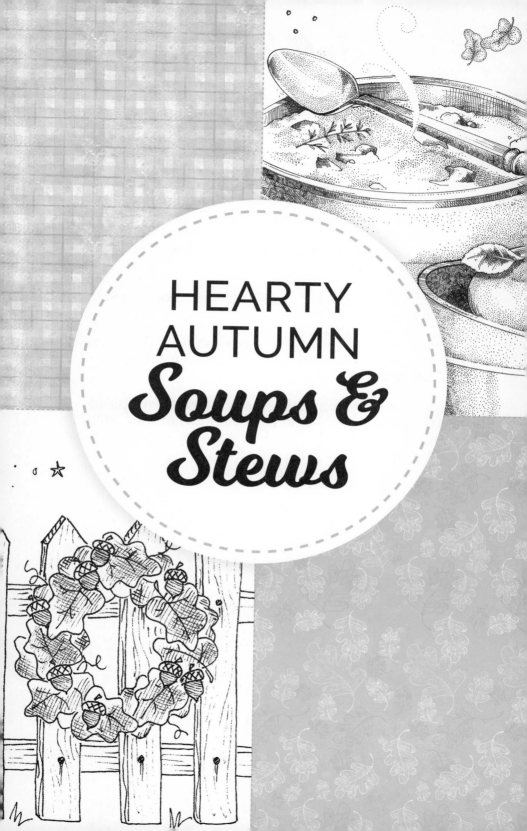

HEARTY AUTUMN
Soups & Stews

Sarah's Halloween Night Pumpkin Chili

Sarah Cameron
Virginia Beach, VA

I always make this recipe throughout October and sometimes November! I loved to make it before my kids went trick-or-treating. Then they would have a hearty, healthy meal to come home to, before they devoured their Halloween candy. My little ghosts and goblins loved it!

1-1/2 lbs. ground beef
1 onion, chopped
2 14-1/2 oz. cans diced
   tomatoes
2 16-oz. cans pinto beans
15-oz. can pumpkin

1-1/4 oz. pkg. chili seasoning
   mix
1 t. pumpkin pie spice
Garnish: sour cream, shredded
   Cheddar cheese

In a large soup pot over medium heat, brown beef with onion, about 10 minutes. Drain; stir in tomatoes with juice and remaining ingredients except garnish. Reduce heat to low. Simmer for about one hour, stirring occasionally. Serves 6.

Take a harvest-time family outing to a farm. Many are open to the public for good old-fashioned fun like pumpkin picking, corn mazes and hayrides. You'll enjoy it as much as the kids!

HEARTY AUTUMN
Soups & Stews

Sausage, Chicken & Orzo Soup

Kay Daugherty
Collinsville, MS

Every fall, my husband and I love to make soup together. We concocted this recipe a few years ago out of what we had on hand. It is so nourishing and warming that it is one of our favorites. Serve with fresh-baked whole-wheat rolls or crusty French bread.

1 to 2 T. olive oil
1 onion, chopped
1 clove garlic, minced
1 lb. sweet Italian pork sausage,
    casing removed
2 c. deli rotisserie chicken,
    shredded
8 c. chicken or vegetable broth

15-1/2 oz. can Italian diced
    tomatoes with basil,
    garlic & oregano
Italian seasoning, salt and
    pepper to taste
1 lb. fresh spinach
8-oz. pkg. orzo pasta,
    uncooked

Drizzle olive oil into a large soup pot over medium heat. Add onion; sauté until tender. Add garlic; sauté for about 2 minutes. Add crumbled sausage; cook until sausage begins to brown. Add chicken, broth, tomatoes with juice and seasonings; stir in spinach. Bring to a boil; reduce heat to medium-low. Add orzo and cook until tender, about 12 to 15 minutes. Makes 10 servings.

Tuck a fall floral arrangement of yellow spider mums and orange gerbera daisies into a vintage soup tureen...a whimsical table decoration for a casual supper. Florist foam will hold everything in place.

69

Amish Garden Vegetable Soup

Marcia Shaffer
Conneaut Lake, PA

We live in an area of northwest Pennsylvania that has a large Amish community. I was lucky enough to get this great recipe when my garden was full of fresh vegetables to use. Feel free to add other veggies that you have on hand...just add a little water to cover.

2 to 3 c. tomato juice
1 qt. home-canned beef chunks,
    or 1 lb. ground beef,
    browned and drained
1 c. potatoes, peeled and diced

1 c. onion, chopped
1 c. carrots, peeled and diced
1 c. fresh or frozen peas
1/2 c. celery, chopped
1 t. salt

Combine all ingredients in a 5-quart slow cooker. Cover and cook on low setting for 7 to 8 hours. Makes 6 to 8 servings.

Invite everyone to a soup & sandwich party...perfect for game day!
With a big pot of your heartiest soup or chili simmering on the
stove, a platter of tasty sandwiches and brownies for dessert,
you'll all have time to relax and enjoy the game.

Roasted Butternut Squash Soup

*Sonia Daily
Rochester, MI*

*This soup is best made with fresh farmstand butternut squash.
It always gets rave reviews. Garnish with a sprinkle of
toasted squash seeds, if you like.*

2 butternut squash, halved and
    seeds removed
1 onion, chopped
4 T. butter
4 c. chicken broth

1/2 t. dried marjoram or oregano
1/4 t. pepper
1/4 t. cayenne pepper
2 8-oz. pkgs. cream cheese,
    softened

Place squash halves, cut-side down, on a lightly greased baking sheet.
Bake at 375 degrees for 45 minutes; cool. In a soup pot over medium
heat, cook onion in butter until tender. Add chicken broth and
seasonings. Scoop out squash and add to pot. Simmer for 15 minutes.
Stir in cream cheese. Using a hand-held immersion blender, purée soup
to desired consistency. May also purée in batches in a blender; return
to pot and heat through over low heat. Makes 8 servings.

Make your Jack-o'-Lantern creations last longer! Add a
tablespoon of bleach to a quart of water, then use a soft cloth
to wipe the pumpkin inside & out. Apply a thin layer
of petroleum jelly to the cut surfaces.

White Bean & Kale Soup

Betty Kozlowski
Newnan, GA

My husband and I love this wonderful, flavorful and healthy soup!
It's simple to make, and the aroma is irresistible as it simmers.

1 lb. ground turkey breakfast
  sausage
3 14-oz. cans chicken or
  vegetable broth
16-oz. can Great Northern
  beans, drained and rinsed
15-oz. can tomato purée
3/4 c. onion, chopped

2 cloves garlic, minced
2 t. dried basil
1 lb. fresh kale, coarsely
  chopped
salt and pepper to taste
Garnish: olive oil, grated
  Parmesan cheese

Brown sausage in a large soup pot over medium heat; drain. Add broth, beans, tomato paste, onion, garlic and basil; stir well. Reduce heat to very low. Cover and simmer for 3 to 4 hours, stirring occasionally, to allow flavors to blend. About 30 minutes before serving time, stir in kale, adding in batches as needed. Continue to cook for 20 to 30 minutes, until kale is wilted and tender. Season with salt and pepper. Drizzle servings with olive oil; top with Parmesan cheese. Makes 6 to 8 servings.

I can see the woods in their autumn dress, the oaks purple,
the hickories washed with gold, the maples and
the sumacs luminous with crimson fires.

–Mark Twain

HEARTY AUTUMN
Soups & Stews

Polish Sausage Soup

Phyllis Rack
Hoffman Estates, IL

I grew up at a time when people ate all their meals at home. This is a recipe I have used all my life, married 60 years ago and raising five kids. The recipe is hearty, filling and very easy to double.

2 c. water
2 potatoes, peeled and diced
2 carrots, peeled and sliced
2 stalks celery, chopped
1/2 c. onion, chopped

10-3/4 oz. can bean & bacon soup
1/2 smoked Polish sausage link, sliced

In a large saucepan, bring water to a boil over medium heat. Add vegetables; simmer for 10 minutes, or until vegetables are nearly tender. Stir in soup and sausage. Reduce heat to low. Simmer for another 15 minutes, adding more water if necessary. Makes 6 servings.

In 2015, our family started a brand-new Thanksgiving tradition. That October, my husband and I were saved. For Thanksgiving, we decided to put others before ourselves, volunteering to serve hot Thanksgiving meals to veterans and others who may not be able to travel home for the holidays or may not be able to prepare a Thanksgiving meal at home themselves. This is an annual event in our city that serves meals to over 1,500 people. We were thrilled to be able to give back and help others during the holiday season. Most importantly, we hope to instill in our son the desire to help others and have a servant's heart like the Lord wants us all to do. I hope you all have a wonderfully blessed holiday season too!

–Kristi Flores-Smith, Abilene, TX

Wild Rice & Turkey Soup

Kimberlee Schmidgall
Tremont, IL

Years ago, my aunt cooked up a pot of this soup for a casual family gathering, and it has been a yummy favorite ever since. It's great for those holiday turkey leftovers. My Minnesota cousins help keep us Illinoisans supplied with wild rice!

3/4 c. onion, chopped
2 stalks celery, diced
2 carrots, peeled and diced
1/2 c. butter
1/2 c. all-purpose flour
4 c. chicken broth

2 c. cooked wild rice
2 c. cooked turkey, diced
1 t. dried parsley
1 t. salt
Optional: 1/4 t. pepper
16-oz. container light cream

In a large soup pot over medium heat, sauté onion, celery and carrots in butter until onion is transparent. Reduce heat to medium-low. Blend in flour; cook and stir until bubbly. Gradually add chicken broth, stirring constantly. Bring to a boil; boil for one minute. Reduce heat to low; stir in remaining ingredients. Simmer for 20 minutes, stirring occasionally. Serves 10.

Gather bundles of garden-fresh herbs and tie with raffia. To each bundle, add a little tag that you've written a friend's name on. A fragrant gift and a terrific way to use the last of the herbs still growing in your garden.

Rivel Soup

Barbara Imler
Noblesville, IN

I remember taking this simple soup to school in my thermos in my lunchbox when I was a child. I always liked it, maybe because there weren't any of those pesky vegetables you usually found in soup!

8 c. chicken broth
1 c. all-purpose flour
1/4 t. salt
1 egg yolk, beaten

15-1/4 oz. can corn, drained
Optional: 1/2 to 1 c. cooked
    chicken, diced
salt and pepper to taste

In a soup pot over high heat, bring broth to a boil. Meanwhile, combine flour and salt in a bowl. Add yolk and work together with fingers until mixture is crumbly. Add the crumbs of flour mixture, a few at a time, to the boiling broth. Reduce heat to medium. Stir in corn, seasonings and chicken, if using. Simmer for 10 minutes, or until rivels are cooked. Makes 6 servings.

A friend who's under the weather would love a care basket delivered to her door. Fill it with homemade soup and bread, a good book and a pair of fuzzy socks. Just right for beating a cold!

Lima Bean Soup

Charlotte Smith
Alexandria, PA

This is my grandma's recipe. It's so tasty and makes me so happy when I make it. It brings back so many great memories of the greatest grandmother in the world. This soup takes awhile to make, but it's great to have simmering on a chilly afternoon.

1 lb. dried lima beans, rinsed
    and sorted
1 meaty ham bone or
    2 ham hocks
2-1/2 qts. plus 1 c. water,
    divided
5 carrots, peeled and cut into
    chunks

5 stalks celery, cut into chunks
1 clove garlic, minced
2 T. butter
2 T. all-purpose flour
2 t. salt
1/2 t. pepper
1 c. elbow macaroni, uncooked

Place dried beans in a Dutch oven; add enough water to cover by 2 inches. Bring to a boil over high heat; reduce heat to medium-low and cook for 35 minutes. Remove from heat; let stand for one hour. Drain and discard liquid; return beans to pan. Add ham bone or hocks and 2-1/2 quarts water; bring to a boil. Reduce heat to low. Simmer for 1-1/2 hours, stirring occasionally. Remove ham bone; cut meat into chunks and return to pan. Add carrots and celery. Cover and simmer over low heat for one hour, or until beans are tender. Meanwhile, in a skillet over medium heat, sauté garlic in butter for one minute. Stir in flour, salt and pepper. Add remaining water and bring to a boil. Reduce heat to low; cook and stir for 2 minutes, or until thickened. Add flour mixture and macaroni to the soup. Simmer for 10 to 12 minutes, until soup is thickened and macaroni is cooked. Serves 12.

Serve up mummy dogs in a jiffy...perfect for kids before they set out to trick-or-treat! For each, wrap a strip of bread stick dough around a hot dog. Arrange them on an ungreased baking sheet and bake at 375 degrees for 12 to 15 minutes.

HEARTY AUTUMN
Soups & Stews

Chicken Corn Chowder

Kevin Eagleton
Greenwood, IN

*I used to make this delicious chowder when I was
a cook at a restaurant in Columbus, Indiana.*

8 c. water
1 c. chicken broth
4 c. cooked chicken breasts,
   diced
2 c. potatoes, peeled, cooked
   and diced
2 c. frozen corn

3 c. celery, diced
2 c. milk
1/2 c. light cream
1-1/2 t. kosher salt
1 c. shredded Cheddar cheese
1 c. shredded mozzarella cheese

In a large soup pot over medium heat, bring water and chicken broth
to a boil. Add chicken and vegetables; return to a boil. Cook until
celery is tender. Reduce heat to medium-low; stir in remaining
ingredients. Simmer over low heat until cheese is melted. Makes 12 to
15 servings.

Making a campfire? Here are some quick tips. Crumple newspaper
for the first layer, then add dry twigs. Light the paper, add several
pieces of wood and let it burn down to glowing red coals. Let it
burn down a bit more, then place the cooking grate over the coals.

Taco Chicken Chili

Denise Schwenger
Port Republic, NJ

I love this slow-cooker recipe because I can spend the day with the grandchildren while dinner is cooking. We can come home to a yummy supper, and the clean-up is a snap!

3 to 4 boneless, skinless chicken breasts
1-oz. pkg. ranch salad dressing mix
1-1/4 oz. pkg. taco seasoning mix
3/4 c. onion, diced
14-1/2 oz. can diced tomatoes with green chiles

15-1/2 oz. can black beans
15-1/2 oz. can can cannellini beans
15-1/2 oz. can kidney beans
16-oz. can vegetarian baked beans
15-1/4 oz. can corn, drained
Optional: sour cream, shredded Cheddar cheese

Add all except optional ingredients to a 6-quart slow cooker in order listed. Do not rinse or drain beans; do not stir. Cover and cook on low setting for 6 to 8 hours. Remove chicken to a plate. Shred and return to slow cooker; stir. Serve in deep soup bowls; top with sour cream and cheese, if desired. Makes 6 to 8 servings.

Serving soup to little eaters? Cut out Jack-o'-Lantern faces from cheese slices. Top soup bowls with the cut-out shapes. How fun!

HEARTY AUTUMN
Soups & Stews

Warm-Your-Tummy Bean Soup

Sheri Dulaney
Englewood, OH

This soup is yummy with a batch of cornbread. Great for meals on a chilly day, or for sharing with a friend who is under the weather.

2 48-oz. jars deluxe mixed
   or pinto beans
1 c. frozen chopped onions
8 c. beef broth

10-3/4 oz. can tomato soup
2 14-oz. pkgs. smoked sausage
   links, sliced 1/4-inch thick

In a large soup pot, combine beans, onions and beef broth. Remove 4 cups of mixture to a blender; process until puréed and pour into a bowl. Repeat twice, until 12 cups are puréed. Return puréed mixture to soup pot over high heat. Stir in soup and sausage. Simmer for 15 to 20 minutes, stirring occasionally, until heated through. Serves 16 to 20.

Easy Corn Sticks

Gladys Kielar
Whitehouse, OH

No special pan needed! The family will love these corn sticks when eating homemade chili or soup.

2 c. biscuit baking mix
2 T. green onion, minced

3/4 c. creamed corn
2 T. butter, melted

Combine biscuit mix, green onion and corn in a bowl; stir until well moistened. Place dough on a floured surface; roll out 1/2-inch thick. Cut into 3-inch by one-inch strips. Roll strips in melted butter; place on an ungreased baking sheet. Bake at 400 degrees for 15 minutes, or until golden. Makes 6.

Wrap silverware in napkins, then slip a cookie cutter over each as a clever napkin ring.

Aunt Joan's Cabbage Patch Soup

Sharon Jones
Oklahoma City, OK

My Aunt Joan from Tulsa, Oklahoma makes this soup all the time. It is filling and delicious, good any time of the year. This soup freezes well, so make a double batch and save time another day.

1 lb. ground beef
1 onion, chopped
1 green pepper, chopped
1/2 c. celery, chopped
15-1/2 oz. can diced tomatoes
15-1/2 oz. can kidney beans,
    drained

15-1/2 oz. can chili beans,
    drained
salt and pepper to taste
2 to 3 c. cabbage, finely
    shredded

Combine beef, onion, green pepper and celery in a large skillet over medium heat. Cook until beef is browned and vegetables are soft; drain. Add tomatoes with juice, beans, salt and pepper. Bring to a boil. Reduce heat to medium-low. Add cabbage, pushing cabbage just under the liquid. Cover and simmer for about 20 to 30 minutes, stirring occasionally. This soup freezes well. Makes 4 to 6 servings.

Gather the last of the garden veggies to freeze and enjoy throughout the winter. Slice or cube carrots, onions, corn, squash and tomatoes. Combine them in gallon-size plastic zipping bags... flavorful stews and soups will be ready in no time!

HEARTY AUTUMN
Soups & Stews

Porcupine Stew

Robin Hill
Rochester, NY

My family likes to make this stew whenever we go camping. The first time I served it, my kids were a little worried, but I reassured them that it doesn't really have porcupine in it! When we camp, I make the meatballs and tuck them in the cooler, then brown them and make the stew in camp.

3 lbs. ground beef
2 6.8-oz. pkgs. beef-flavored
    rice vermicelli mix, uncooked
1 onion, chopped
1/2 c. instant mashed potato
    flakes
3 eggs, beaten

5 c. water
15-1/2 oz. can diced tomatoes
14-1/2 oz. can cut green beans
15-1/4 oz. can corn
5 potatoes, peeled and diced
1 lb. baby carrots, sliced

In a large bowl, combine beef, rice vermicelli mixes with flavor packets, onion, potato flakes and eggs. Mix well; form into one-inch meatballs. Brown meatballs in a Dutch oven over medium heat. Add water; bring to a boil. Reduce heat to medium-low and simmer for 30 minutes. Add remaining ingredients; do not drain cans. Simmer for another 30 minutes, or until vegetables are tender. Serves 10.

Don't wait 'til Thanksgiving to use your festive holiday dishes...
use them all season long for a daily dose of cheer!

All-Day Beef Barley Soup

Rosemary Lightbown
Wakefield, RI

This slow-cooker soup is especially delicious when served
with warm bread and shredded Parmesan cheese.

2 lbs. stew beef cubes
2 T. olive oil
1 onion, chopped
2 cloves garlic, minced
2 15-1/2 oz. cans diced
    tomatoes
32-oz. container beef broth
8-oz. can tomato sauce
2/3 c. corn

1 red or green pepper, chopped
3/4 c. green beans, trimmed and
    cut into 1-inch pieces
2/3 c. long-cooking barley,
    uncooked
1 t. salt
1/4 t. pepper
Optional: 1/2 t. dried thyme

In a large skillet over medium heat, brown beef cubes on all sides in
olive oil. Add onion and garlic; sauté for several minutes, until onion
is tender. Drain; transfer beef mixture to a 6-quart slow cooker. Add
tomatoes with juice and remaining ingredients; stir to mix. Cover and
cook on low setting for 7 to 8 hours, until beef, vegetables and barley
are tender. Makes 8 servings.

I cannot endure to waste anything as precious as
autumn sunshine by staying in the house. So I spend
almost all the daylight hours in the open air.

–Nathaniel Hawthorne

Family Favorite Biscuits

Ellie Barton
Colville, WA

My family loves these biscuits! They are so simple and easy to make, and I can whip up a batch really quick. They go very well with soup. This recipe can be used to make strawberry shortcakes too. Just add 1/4 to 1/3 cup sugar to the flour mixture.

1 c. all-purpose flour
1 c. whole-wheat flour
2 t. baking powder
1/2 t. baking soda
1/2 t. salt

1 egg, beaten
5 to 6 T. milk
1/3 c. butter, melted and
    cooled slightly

In a large bowl, mix flours, baking powder, baking soda and salt. Make a well in the center; set aside. In a measuring cup, combine beaten egg and enough milk to equal 2/3 cup. Stir in melted butter. Add egg mixture to the well in flour mixture. Stir just until combined; do not overmix. Turn out dough onto a lightly floured surface. Knead dough 3 to 5 times, until smooth and uniform. Pat into a circle, 1/2-inch to 3/4-inch thick. Cut out dough with a biscuit cutter; place on a greased baking sheet. Biscuits should be just touching, not pressed together. Bake at 350 degrees for 10 to 12 minutes, until lightly golden and flaky. Makes one dozen.

Ladle 2-cup portions of leftover soup into freezer bags... seal, label and freeze. Then, when you need a quick-fix dinner, simply let family members choose a bag. Transfer soup to a microwave-safe bowl and reheat.

One-Hour Wild Rice Soup

Lindsey Ellingsen
Milton, WA

My mom used to make this soup for us during cold weather. Once I made it for my husband when I was feeling a little homesick, and he said, "Why on earth have we never had this before?!" Now he asks for this soup all through autumn and winter. It tastes wonderful served in sourdough bread bowls.

1 c. wild rice, uncooked	1 green pepper, chopped
32-oz. container chicken or	2 t. jalapeño pepper, minced
vegetable broth	1 t. dried rosemary
1 T. olive oil	1 t. dried thyme
3 stalks celery, chopped	pepper to taste
3 carrots, peeled and chopped	2 23-oz. cans cream of
1/2 c. onion, chopped	mushroom soup

Cook wild rice in broth, according to package directions. This may take from 45 to 55 minutes at a simmer. Do not drain. Meanwhile, warm olive oil in a soup pot over medium-high heat. Add celery, carrots, onion and peppers; sauté until crisp-tender. Add seasonings, cooked rice and soup to vegetables. Cook, stirring often, until bubbly and heated through. Serves 4 to 6.

After dinner, enjoy some Halloween storytelling outside around a fire or inside by candlelight...frightfully fun!

HEARTY AUTUMN
Soups & Stews

Irish Potato Soup

Shirley Condy
Plainview, NY

This recipe is from my Irish family members. So easy and so good!

4 slices bacon
4 c. potatoes, peeled and diced
1 c. onion, chopped
4 c. chicken broth

4 c. water
1 c. whipping cream
salt and pepper to taste
Garnish: chopped fresh parsley

In a large saucepan over medium heat, cook bacon until crisp. Remove bacon to a paper towel, reserving drippings in pan. Sauté potatoes and onion for 5 minutes in reserved drippings. Add chicken broth and water; bring to a boil. Reduce heat to medium-low; simmer until potatoes are tender. Stir in seasonings and cream. Heat through but do not boil. At serving time, garnish with crumbled bacon and parsley. Makes 6 to 8 servings.

Each year, as September dawns, my sister Eileen and I enjoy the excitement of kicking off several months of special family gatherings. Since we live in Florida (next door to each other!) and the weather is still very warm in fall, we create the cozy feeling that fall brings by transforming our homes into a colorful display of orange and gold leaves and garlands, complete with lights. We have several family birthdays in September, and the celebrations would not be complete without pumpkins, scarecrows and fall table linens. My granddaughter even wrote about these celebrations in a college essay...she shared some of our family traditions that help her to remember that there is still goodness and love in this world. Although we are teased by our grown kids, we know that they look forward to the fuss, and our grandkids will have many enjoyable memories to take with them as they grow.

–Muriel Vlahakis, Sarasota, FL

Southwest Beef Stew

Shirley Howie
Foxboro, MA

This delicious slow-cooker recipe adds a distinct southwest flavor to ordinary beef stew. This is a very easy everyday recipe, but is impressive enough for casual entertaining.

1 lb. stew beef cubes
3/4 c. onion, chopped
28-oz. can whole tomatoes
1 t. chili powder
1 t. dried basil
1-1/4 oz. pkg. taco seasoning
    mix

15-oz. can black beans, drained
    and rinsed
11-oz. can sweet corn & diced
    peppers, drained

Combine beef cubes, onion, tomatoes with juice, chili powder and basil in a 4-quart slow cooker. Cover and cook on low setting for 8 to 9 hours, until beef is tender. Stir in taco seasoning, beans and corn. Cover and cook on high setting for 15 to 30 minutes, until bubbly and thickened. Makes 4 servings.

On clear, crisp autumn days, freshen household quilts and blankets for winter. Simply shake them out and spread over a porch rail or fence. Sunshine and fresh air will quickly chase away any mustiness that they've picked up in storage.

Can't-Miss Cornbread

Lori Thoman
Orem, UT

My husband loves this cornbread. It reminds him of his grandmother. No dry cornbread here! It is moist, and tastes amazing with honey butter...or even without anything else at all.

2 c. buttermilk
4 eggs, beaten
1-1/3 c. sugar
1 c. butter, melted and cooled
    slightly

1-1/4 c. cornmeal
2-3/4 c. all-purpose flour
1-1/2 t. baking powder
1/2 t. baking soda
1 t. salt

In a large bowl, whisk together buttermilk, eggs, sugar and melted butter; set aside. In a separate bowl, mix remaining ingredients. Add cornmeal mixture to buttermilk mixture; stir until just mixed. Batter will be lumpy. Pour batter into a lightly greased 13"x9" baking pan. Bake at 375 degrees for 35 minutes. Cut into squares. Makes 2 dozen servings.

Whip up some back-to-school clipboards to show off the children's best artwork, bragging-rights school papers and other special items. Decorate dollar-store clipboards with paint, add each child's name with wooden game tiles and hang up the clipboards on nails. It's that simple!

Pasta Minestrone Soup

Karen Ellen Mills
Midland, MI

I love a fresh pot of homemade soup! Cooler weather encourages me to find my best slow-cooker recipes and get ready for several months of comfort food. This soup freezes well and can be warmed up quickly for another meal another day.

2 15-1/2 oz. cans diced
   tomatoes
32-oz. container chicken broth
2 potatoes, peeled and cubed
1 to 2 carrots, peeled and
   chopped
1 to 2 stalks celery, chopped
4 green onions, sliced
1/2 c. frozen peas

1 T. red wine vinegar
1 t. Italian seasoning
cayenne pepper to taste
1/2 c. small shell pasta,
   uncooked
1/2 c. romaine lettuce, chopped
Garnish: grated Parmesan
   cheese, chopped fresh
   parsley

In a 5-quart slow cooker, combine tomatoes with juice, broth, vegetables, vinegar and seasonings. Cover and cook on low setting for 6 to 7 hours, or on high setting for 5 hours. During the last 20 minutes of cooking time, stir in uncooked pasta; place lettuce on top. Cover and cook for the last 20 minutes. Serve in large soup bowls, topped with cheese and parsley. This soup freezes well. Serves 6 to 8.

For an autumn centerpiece that only takes a moment, place a shapely pumpkin on a cake stand and tuck some bittersweet sprigs around it. Simple, yet so eye-catching.

HEARTY AUTUMN
Soups & Stews

5-Can Veggie Soup

Diana Chaney
Olathe, KS

*This soup is ready in a jiffy...just mix, heat and serve! Sometimes
I'll add some leftover chopped chicken, or even sliced hot dogs...
that's how the kids like it! But it's good just the way it is.*

19-oz. can minestrone soup
15-1/2 oz. can diced tomatoes
15-1/4 oz. can corn

15-oz. can mixed vegetables
15-1/2 oz. can black beans,
   drained and rinsed

Combine all ingredients in a large saucepan; drain only the beans. Heat
through over medium heat, about 10 minutes. Serves 6.

Many years ago, my husband and I and our two children, my mom
& dad, my younger siblings and their families would go on an
autumn outing in October. We would meet at Lincoln City State
Park in southern Indiana, near where Abraham Lincoln lived as a
boy. Visiting this park was a wonderful way to reacquaint ourselves
with nature. The autumn colors displayed their finest array and the
locusts and birds sang, making it a joyous reunion of sight and
sound. The cool nip in the air felt so good after the steamy days
of summer. We all contributed to a picnic lunch in a meadow in
the park, feasting on fried chicken, apples, cheese, chips, cookies,
cider and other goodies. We would play tag or hide & seek, take
hikes in the woods and have a wonderful time. Our families are
mostly grown now, and Dad left us after a stroke in 2008. Dad
really enjoyed this outing and having his family all together,
enjoying the fruits of the earth. Going back for a family gathering
now wouldn't be the same without him. I think these times are
best kept in our memories as some of the best times of our lives.

–Barbara Klein, Newburgh, IN

That Good Soup

*Becky Sherrill
Bolivar, TN*

*Whenever I ask my husband what he wants me to fix to eat, he does
not hesitate...his answer is always, "That soup, the good kind that
I love." He would eat this seven days a week! It is delicious, especially
on a crisp, cold night when you want something easy to prepare. The
hot sauce give it the bite that it needs. Serve with cornbread or a
basket of saltine crackers.*

1-1/2 lbs. ground beef chuck
1 onion, chopped
6 c. potatoes, peeled and cubed
3 8-oz. cans tomato sauce, or
    more to taste
4 c. chicken broth

2 c. water
2 t. kosher salt
1 t. pepper
1/2 to 1 t. hot pepper sauce,
    to taste
Garnish: chopped fresh parsley

In a Dutch oven over medium heat, brown beef with onion; drain. Add
remaining ingredients except parsley; stir. Bring to a boil over medium-
high heat. Reduce heat to medium-low. Simmer for one hour, or until
potatoes are tender but not overcooked. Garnish servings with a
sprinkle of parsley. Makes 8 to 10 servings.

Welcome autumn with a new wreath on the front door! Decorate a
purchased wreath form with fallen leaves, clusters of seed pods,
nuts, ornamental grasses and other fall finds. A terrific way to
enjoy items collected on a leaf-peeping walk! Simply attach the
fall finds with florist pins or hot glue.

Vermont Maple Cornbread

Shirley Howie
Foxboro, MA

I grew up on a small farm in Vermont, and we made maple syrup every spring in our little sugarhouse that sat at the edge of the woods. Mom was always looking for new ways to use our syrup, and this one was one of our favorites. Try it topped with a drizzle of warm maple syrup for extra maple flavor...so good!

1-1/3 c. all-purpose flour
2/3 c. cornmeal
1 T. baking powder
1/2 t. salt

1 c. milk
1/3 c. pure maple syrup
1/4 c. butter, melted
2 eggs, lightly beaten

In a large bowl, combine flour, cornmeal, baking powder and salt; mix well. Add remaining ingredients; stir just until combined. Batter will be lumpy; do not overmix. Pour batter into a greased 8"x8" baking pan. Bake at 400 degrees for 25 to 30 minutes, until golden and a toothpick inserted in the center tests clean. Cut into squares; serve warm. Makes 9 servings.

Honey-Maple Biscuits

Andrea Heyart
Savannah, TX

I gussied up a recipe from an old Ozark cookbook I had and came up with these yummy biscuits. Delicious warm with honey butter!

2 c. all-purpose flour
1 c. sugar
1 t. baking soda
1/2 t. salt
1 c. sour cream

1 c. butter, softened
1/2 c. honey
1/2 c. pure maple syrup
1 egg, beaten

Combine all ingredients in a large bowl; mix well. Add batter to 24 well-greased muffin cups, filling 2/3 full. Bake at 350 degrees for 25 minutes, or until tops are golden. Makes 2 dozen.

Linda's White Chicken Chili

Diana Krol
Hutchinson, KS

Our friend Linda shared this delicious slow-cooker soup with our family several years ago. It's been served in assorted family homes ever since. It makes a lot, so it's perfect for gatherings.

5 c. cooked chicken, chopped or shredded
3 15-1/2 oz. cans Great Northern beans, rinsed and drained
32-oz. container chicken broth
16-oz. jar salsa

8-oz. pkg. shredded Pepper Jack cheese
2 t. ground cumin
2 cloves garlic, minced
salt and pepper to taste
Garnish: sour cream, corn chips

Combine all ingredients except garnish in a 6-quart slow cooker. Stir gently. Cover and cook on high setting for about 2 hours, until hot, bubbly and cheese has melted. Garnish servings with sour cream and corn chips. Makes 10 to 12 servings.

Garnish individual servings of soup with a sour cream "spiderweb." Spoon sour cream into a plastic zipping bag. Snip a tiny corner from the bag and pipe sour cream on the soup in circles. Run a knife tip through the sour cream several times, from the center to the edge of the bowl, to resemble a spiderweb.

HEARTY AUTUMN
Soups & Stews

Quick Tamale Stew

Linda Storer
Taylorsville, UT

This is a recipe for when you're short on time. Kids love it!

14-1/2 oz. can tamales
14-1/2 oz. can chili
14-1/2 oz. can diced tomatoes
14-1/2 oz. can corn, drained

Optional: 2-1/4 oz. can sliced
   black olives, drained
Garnish: shredded Cheddar
   cheese, sour cream

Unwrap tamales; cut into bite-size pieces. In a saucepan, combine tamales, chili, tomatoes with juice, corn and olives, if using. Cook over medium heat until hot and bubbly, 10 to 15 minutes. Garnish servings with cheese or sour cream. Makes 4 servings.

Easy Chicken Tortilla Soup

Robyn Stroh
Calera, AL

This is a easy and healthy soup that is quick to toss together.
Instead of the cooked chicken, you can use a deli rotisserie chicken,
pulled from the bone and coarsely chopped.

4 chicken breasts, cooked
   and shredded
32-oz. container chicken broth
16-oz. jar salsa
15-1/2 oz. can cannellini beans,
   rinsed and drained

Garnish: shredded Cheddar
   cheese, crushed tortilla chips,
   sliced green onions

Add all ingredients except garnish to a 4-quart slow cooker; give a quick stir. Cover and cook on low setting for 8 to 10 hours, or on high setting for 4 to 6 hours. Top servings with cheese, crushed chips and onions. Serves 6 to 8.

Spoon hot tomato soup into a thermos and bring it along to the high school football game...sure to take the chill right off!

Bonnie's Chicken Noodle Soup

Sharon Alexander
Independence, MO

This is my mom's recipe...she's an awesome cook! She loves to cook for people, to help them in time of need or just to bless them for no special reason at all. I've fixed this soup for co-workers, friends at church and other family members, and everyone raves about how delicious it is. So to honor her and her giving spirit, I wanted to share this recipe for everyone to enjoy.

3 boneless, skinless chicken breasts
chicken & poultry seasoning
salt to taste
3 10-1/2 oz. cans chicken broth
4 c. water
2 cubes chicken bouillon
1/2 t. curry powder
1 t. garlic salt, or more to taste
10 baby carrots, chopped
1/4 c. onion, chopped
1 stalk celery, chopped
12-oz. pkg. extra broad no-yolk noodles, uncooked
3 10-3/4 oz. cans cream of chicken soup

Season chicken lightly on all sides with chicken seasoning. Arrange chicken in a lightly greased 13"x9" baking pan. Bake, uncovered, at 400 degrees for 20 to 25 minutes, until chicken juices run clear; set aside to cool. Meanwhile, combine chicken broth, water and bouillon cubes in a large soup pot. Bring to a boil over high heat; season with curry powder and garlic salt. Reduce heat to medium. Add vegetables; simmer until partially tender. Add noodles; cook until tender. Dice baked chicken and add to broth. Stir in chicken soup; add more water to desired consistency, if too thick. Simmer for a few more minutes. Serves 8 to 10.

If you're hosting a backyard soup supper, toss a few colorful quilts and throws over the chairs. So cozy for snuggling under as the sun sets!

HEARTY AUTUMN
Soups & Stews

Chicken, Spinach & Orzo Soup

Becky Butler
Keller, TX

This is one of my go-to recipes when I have cooked chicken left over from another meal. Instead of the cooked chicken, you can use a 12-ounce can of chunk white chicken, including the broth.

3 T. olive oil
2/3 c. leeks, sliced, white and
   pale green parts only
1 c. carrots, peeled and finely
   diced
1/2 t. dried oregano
2 32-oz. containers reduced-
   sodium chicken broth
1 c. yellow squash, diced

2 T. fresh parsley, chopped
zest of 1 lemon
1 c. cooked chicken, shredded
1 c. cooked orzo pasta or other
   small soup pasta
1/2 t. salt
1/2 t. pepper
8-oz. pkg. baby spinach

Heat olive oil in a stockpot over medium-high heat; add leeks, carrots and oregano. Sauté until leeks are wilted, about 3 to 4 minutes. Add chicken broth and bring to a simmer. Add remaining ingredients except spinach; stir. Cook for 5 to 10 minutes, until squash is tender. Add spinach by handfuls. Cook and stir until spinach is wilted and tender, 2 to 3 minutes. Serves 8.

Cook up a big pot of chicken to freeze for later. For juicy, flavorful chicken, cover with water and simmer gently until cooked through, then turn off the heat and let the chicken cool in its own broth. Shred or cube chicken, wrap well in recipe-size portions and freeze.

Grandma's Amazing Beef Stew

Kristen Berning
Otsego, MN

My grandma and mom were known for sharing this simple, no-fail dish when hosting Sunday dinners for family & friends. If you are in a hurry, most grocery stores sell these fresh vegetables pre-cut and packed together in a bag. A perfect and easy supper awaits you and your family!

1 lb. stew beef cubes
1 c. celery, chopped
3/4 c. onion, chopped
2 c. carrots, peeled and chopped
4 potatoes, peeled and cubed
2 T. tapioca, uncooked

1 T. sugar
seasoning salt and pepper
   to taste
10-3/4 oz. can tomato soup
1-1/4 c. water

Spray a 5-quart slow cooker with a non-stick vegetable spray. Layer ingredients in the following order: beef cubes, celery, onion, carrots and potatoes. Sprinkle tapioca, sugar and seasonings over top. Spoon soup over all; drizzle with water. Cover and cook on low setting for about 5 hours, until beef is very tender. Makes 4 to 6 servings.

A wire basket full of birch logs is a handy seasonal accent for the fireplace.

HEARTY AUTUMN
Soups & Stews

Nannie's Applesauce Muffins

Susan Shumate
Daleville, VA

It was so much fun to watch my grandmother make these muffins. This recipes bring back fond memories of hearing my granddaddy playing his guitar while waiting to bite into this treat.

4 c. all-purpose flour
2 t. baking soda
1 c. butter, softened
2 eggs, beaten
2 c. sugar

2 c. applesauce
1 T. cinnamon
2 t. ground allspice
1 t. ground cloves
Optional: 1 c. chopped nuts

Combine all ingredients except nuts in a large bowl. Beat well with an electric mixer on medium speed. Add nuts last, if desired. Spoon batter into 24 to 36 well-greased muffin cups, filling 2/3 full. Bake at 400 degrees for 12 to 15 minutes, until tops are well done. Batter may be covered and kept refrigerated for several days; bake a few muffins at a time, as desired. Makes 2 to 3 dozen.

It was a beautiful sunset wedding on Halloween weekend. Jen, the bride, was dressed in a Cinderella Princess costume and the groom, my husband's nephew Steve, was Prince Charming. The wedding guests all wore Halloween costumes as they were escorted to a small area overlooking a lake just before sunset. There were autumn and Halloween decorations, with hay bales neatly stacked up for the seating. After the ceremony, there was a traditional wedding reception dinner of food served buffet style. The band played all kinds of music. After dinner, there was a costume contest and everyone enjoyed looking at all of the different costumes. This turned out to be such a fun wedding with a great group of family & friends...very memorable and unique! The bride and groom are living happily ever after. This Halloween they celebrate their tenth anniversary!

–Karla Himpelmann, Mount Pleasant, MI

Fall Family
·RECIPES·

Cheddar-Ham Chowder

Lori Broderick
Plattsburg, MO

A friend gave me this recipe, and the first time I made it for my family, they licked the pan clean. No leftovers! Since then, I double the recipe when I make it, because it makes a great lunch too.

2 c. water
2 c. potatoes, peeled and cubed
1/2 c. celery, sliced
1/2 c. carrots, peeled and sliced
1/2 c. onion, chopped
1 t. salt
1/2 t. pepper

1/4 c. butter
1/4 c. all-purpose flour
2 c. milk
8-oz. container shredded sharp
    Cheddar cheese
15-1/4 oz. can corn
1-1/2 c. cooked ham, cubed

In a large saucepan over medium-high heat, bring water to a boil. Add potatoes, celery, carrots, onion, salt and pepper. Reduce heat to medium-low. Cover and simmer for 8 to 10 minutes, just until vegetables are tender. Remove from heat; do not drain. Meanwhile, in a medium saucepan over medium heat, melt butter. Blend in flour; add milk all at once. Cook and stir until thickened and bubbly. Add cheese; stir until melted. Add milk mixture to vegetable mixture in large saucepan; stir well. Add corn and ham. Heat through over medium heat, stirring occasionally. Makes 4 servings.

Take the kids to a paint-your-own pottery shop! Let them decorate cheery soup bowls for the whole family. Their creations will warm hearts and tummies at the same time.

HEARTY AUTUMN
Soups & Stews

Split Pea Soup

Janae Mallonee
Marlboro, MA

My daughter is such an odd eater...she loves spinach, lima beans, cabbage, pickled beets and tofu! She doesn't care for scallops or lobster, however. This makes for a much smaller grocery bill! When she was very little, she came to me and asked me to make split pea soup for her. This recipe is the one we came up with together. To this day, it's still her favorite. She is an awesome kitchen helper!

6 c. water
1 lb. dried split peas, rinsed and
   sorted
1 to 1-1/2 c. cooked ham, diced
1 cube chicken bouillon

1/2 c. onion, diced
1/2 c. carrot, peeled and
   shredded
2 cloves garlic, minced
salt and pepper to taste

Add all ingredients except salt and pepper to a large soup pot. Bring to a boil over medium-high heat; reduce heat to medium-low. Cover and cook for about 1-1/2 hours, until peas become mushy and carrots are well dissolved into the soup. Season with salt and pepper. Makes 6 to 8 servings.

Watch for old-fashioned clear glass canisters at tag sales and flea markets...perfect countertop storage for macaroni, pasta and dried beans.

Thanksgiving Leftovers Soup

Vickie
Gooseberry Patch

This recipe is great for using up odds & ends after Thanksgiving. It's very flexible...if you have some leftover broccoli in cheese sauce or a bit of corn casserole, go ahead and use it! This recipe is meatless, but by all means, add some chopped turkey or a sprinkle of crispy bacon too. If you're really bored with leftovers, this soup freezes well. On a cold day in January, pull it out and enjoy it.

3/4 c. onion, diced
3/4 c. celery, diced
2 to 3 t. olive oil
4 c. chicken broth
2 c. mashed potatoes
1/4 to 1/2 c. cooked broccoli or
    cauliflower

1/4 to 1/2 c. corn
1 c. shredded sharp Cheddar
    cheese
1/2 t. paprika
1/2 t. salt
1/4 t. pepper

In a large soup pot over medium heat, sauté onion and celery in oil for 3 to 5 minutes. Add broth; simmer for 6 to 8 minutes. Stir in mashed potatoes; return to a simmer. Using a hand-held immersion blender, purée soup until smooth. Stir in remaining ingredients. Heat through over low heat until bubbly and cheese is melted. Makes 4 to 6 servings.

Pull out your oversize coffee mugs when serving soups, stews, chili, even mains and desserts. They're just right for sharing hearty servings, and the handles make them so easy to hold onto.

FRESH-PICKED
Sides & Salads

Momma Sophie's Zucchini

Isabel Nieves
Santa Ana, CA

This was my mom's recipe that she passed on to us. We love it, and I hope you will too. It's very simple but with lots of flavor.

1 t. olive oil
5 to 6 zucchini, sliced
1/2 yellow onion, chopped
1/4 c. chopped green chiles
1 t. garlic, minced

11-oz. can corn, drained,
  or 1 c. frozen corn
salt and pepper to taste
1/2 c. shredded sharp Cheddar
  cheese

Heat oil in a skillet over medium heat. Add zucchini, onion, chiles and garlic; sauté for about 2 minutes. Add corn, salt and pepper. Cover and cook for 10 to 15 minutes, until zucchini is tender. Uncover and top with cheese. Cover and cook for one more minute, or until cheese is melted. Makes 4 servings.

On a beautiful fall day, have a harvest feast outdoors. Set up
a table under the trees, or turn it into a barn party. Layer woolen
blankets on the table, then mix & match painted chairs
for seating. Make dinner fun!

FRESH-PICKED
Sides & Salads

Karen's Corn Pudding

Karen Gervais
Troy, NY

My family loves this side dish...I make it for most of our holiday dinner get-togethers. I like to freeze my own corn during the summer, when corn is fresh from the farmers' market. I blanch the cobs, scrape the kernels off the cob, pack them in freezer bags and freeze. So much better flavor than store-bought corn!

4 c. frozen corn, thawed
   and drained
3 T. all-purpose flour
2 T. sugar
2 T. butter, melted

1 t. salt, or to taste
pepper to taste
2 eggs, well beaten
1/2 to 2/3 c. milk

In a bowl, combine corn, flour, sugar, melted butter, salt and pepper. Mix well; add eggs and stir again. Stir in milk until thinned but not watery. Spoon corn mixture into a buttered 13"x9" baking pan. Bake, uncovered, at 350 degrees for 45 minutes, or until custard-like and set in the center. Serves 8.

Look for colorful old-fashioned cut flowers like zinnias and dwarf sunflowers at farmers' markets or even your neighborhood supermarket. Arrange a generous bunch in a tall stoneware crock for a cheery centerpiece in no time at all.

Grandma's Green Bean Casserole

Lisa Vyner
Raleigh, NC

As a child, I was lucky enough to live next door to my Grandma Aaron. My fondest childhood memories include the times we spent cooking and baking together, especially at the holidays. Christmas dinner wasn't complete without her green bean casserole on the table.

3 10-oz. pkgs. frozen French-
    cut green beans
3/4 c. onion, chopped
4 t. butter
1 to 2 t. sugar

1 t. paprika
1 t. salt
1-1/2 c. sour cream, divided
12-oz. pkg. sliced Swiss cheese,
    divided

Cook green beans according to package directions; drain. Meanwhile, in a skillet over medium heat, sauté onion in butter. Add sugar, paprika and salt to onion; cook and stir until sugar dissolves. Remove from heat. In a greased 2-quart casserole dish, layer 1/3 each of beans, onion mixture, sour cream and cheese slices. Repeat layers 2 more times, ending with cheese on top. Cover and bake at 350 degrees for 20 to 25 minutes, until bubbly and cheese is melted. Serves 6 to 8.

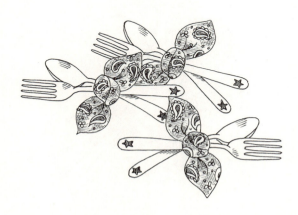

Give tonight's table a little flair...knot a cheery bandanna around each set of flatware. Bandannas come in so many bright colors, everyone can choose their own favorite.

FRESH-PICKED
Sides & Salads

Shredded Brussels Sprouts & Bacon

Joshua Logan
Victoria, TX

No one in my family liked Brussels sprouts until I tried this recipe. Now we're all fans!

2 slices bacon
1/2 c. yellow onion, thinly sliced
1/4 t. salt
3/4 c. water

1 t. Dijon mustard
1 lb. Brussels sprouts, trimmed
  and very thinly sliced
1 T. cider vinegar

In a skillet over medium heat cook bacon until crisp. Drain bacon on a paper towel, reserving drippings. Add onion and salt to drippings. Cook, stirring often, until tender and golden. Stir in water and mustard, scraping up any browned bits. Add Brussels sprouts. Cook, stirring often, until tender, 4 to 6 minutes. Stir in vinegar; top with crumbled bacon. Serves 6.

Broccoli & Cheese Bake

Anne Girucky
Cape Coral, FL

An easy and tasty recipe.

2 10-oz. pkgs. frozen chopped
  broccoli
2 eggs, beaten
2 T. all-purpose flour

8-oz. pkg. shredded Cheddar
  cheese
2 T. butter, melted
salt and pepper to taste

Cook broccoli according to package directions, just until tender; drain. Combine eggs, flour and cheese; mix well and fold in broccoli. Spread melted butter in a 1-1/2 quart casserole dish. Add broccoli mixture. Bake, uncovered, at 350 degrees for 25 to 30 minutes, until set and cheese is melted. Makes 8 servings.

Get kids to eat their veggies! Serve fresh cut-up vegetables with small cups of creamy salad dressing, peanut butter or hummus for dunking.

Twice-Baked Potato Bake

Jennifer Martin
Hope, AR

Ready-to-use bacon bits and skin-on potatoes
make this tasty dish a snap to assemble!

2 lbs. redskin potatoes, cut into
    1/2-inch cubes
1 T. olive oil
1 t. chili powder
1/2 t. seasoned salt
1/4 t. pepper
1/2 c. light ranch salad dressing
1 c. shredded Cheddar cheese
1/2 c. real bacon bits

Lightly spray a 9"x9" baking pan with non-stick vegetable spray. Add potatoes to pan; toss with olive oil. Sprinkle with seasonings and mix again. Cover with aluminum foil. Bake at 400 degrees for 45 minutes. Uncover; stir in salad dressing, cheese and bacon. Bake, uncovered, 10 more minutes, or until cheese is bubbly. Serves 8.

My mom & dad met when they were both teaching elementary school. After they married and had me, my parents decided Mom would stay home from work to raise me and, seven years later, my sister. Mom's homemade, educational games and neighborhood field trips had us knowing colors, shapes, letters and numbers even before we entered kindergarten! Once we did, our tradition was born. Every school-loving kid (and mom) knows that the best day of the year is the last week of August each year...back-to-school shopping. The three of us would get up in the morning, lists in hand, and race to the store. We'd spend hours sharing and laughing and then leave with our arms chock-full of new waxy crayons, markers and pairs of black patent leather shoes. Then, off to the local Chinese restaurant for lunch. Now, my sister & I are both teachers ourselves. Wherever we are, we come back home the last week of August for back-to-school shopping and Chinese food for lunch. Happy to say it's been 28 years and counting!

–Allison Mohler, East Hampton, CT

Creamy Baked Acorn Squash

Becky Drees
Pittsfield, MA

We love acorn squash in the fall. It's delicious and smells dreamy while it's baking. Sometimes I use fresh rosemary instead of thyme, and it's just as tasty.

2 acorn squash, halved and
    seeds removed
1 clove garlic, minced
1 t. fresh thyme, chopped
salt and pepper to taste

1 T. butter, cut into 4 pieces
4 T. whipping cream, divided
4 T. shredded Parmesan cheese,
    divided

Place squash halves cut-side up on a lightly greased baking sheet. Sprinkle with garlic and seasonings. Add a piece of butter and one tablespoon cream to each half. Bake, uncovered, at 375 degrees for 20 minutes. Dip a basting brush into butter mixture in squash halves; brush over cut edges of squash. Bake another 20 minutes. Sprinkle one tablespoon cheese over each squash. Bake for an additional 15 minutes, or until squash is fork-tender. Serves 4.

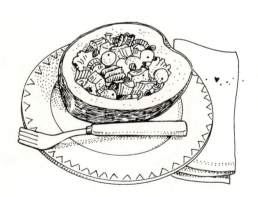

Hard-shelled fall squash can be a challenge to cut for cooking. Do it the easy way! Microwave the whole squash on high setting for 5 minutes. Pierce with a knife tip to check for tenderness and cook a few more minutes as needed. Cool, cut in half and scoop out the seeds...simple!

Steakhouse Creamed Spinach

Kelly Gray
Avon Park, FL

I love the speed and flavor of this recipe. It is so good. I make this any time we are grilling out any type of beef. If I have any leftovers, I use them in an egg omelet in the morning. This takes ten minutes and is very budget-friendly to make.

3 10-oz. pkgs. chopped spinach
1/2 c. butter
2 c. whipping cream or
    half-and-half
1/2 c. all-purpose flour
2 to 3 t. garlic salt

1 t. pepper
1/2 t. nutmeg
1-1/2 c. shredded Swiss cheese
1/2 c. shredded mozzarella
    cheese

Cook spinach according to package directions. Drain; squeeze out all water and return to saucepan. Add butter and cream. Cook over low heat, stirring often, until well blended. Sprinkle with flour and seasonings; mix well. Add cheeses; cook until melted. Serves 6.

Patterned pumpkin centerpieces in no time! Stencil
a favorite pattern on a white Lumina pumpkin or paint
rings of white latex paint around a pale orange
pumpkin to resemble a yellowware bowl.

FRESH-PICKED
Sides & Salads

Tangy Cauliflower

Sandra Commins
Indianapolis, IN

*This is a recipe I picked up in a grocery store many years ago.
I added the dill and Dijon mustard. It is a nice change of pace
from cauliflower in plain cheese sauce.*

1 head cauliflower, cut into
   bite-size flowerets
1/2 c. water
1/2 c. mayonnaise

1-1/2 t. Dijon mustard
1 t. onion, chopped
1 t. fresh dill, snipped
1/2 c. shredded Cheddar cheese

Combine cauliflower and water in a saucepan over medium heat. Cover
and simmer for 10 to 15 minutes, until fork-tender; drain. In a small
bowl, blend mayonnaise, mustard, onion and dill; add to cauliflower
and stir gently. Transfer to a serving dish; sprinkle with cheese. Cover
and let stand a few minutes, until cheese is melted. Serves 4 to 6.

Before displaying gourds and pumpkins as a centerpiece, a quick
wash will help them last longer. Stir together a tablespoon of
bleach in a gallon of water, then gently wash and pat dry.

Easy Mushroom-Rice Pilaf

Shirley Howie
Foxboro, MA

I am always looking for new ways to cook rice, and this recipe is definitely a keeper! It is quick & easy to make and has lots of beefy flavor. It holds its own as a great side dish, but you could also add some leftover cooked beef or pork to it for a quick main dish.

4 T. butter
1 c. onion, chopped
1/2 lb. sliced mushrooms
1-1/2 c. long-cooking rice,
   uncooked

3-1/2 c. water
1-oz. pkg. au jus gravy mix
1/2 t. dried oregano
1/2 t. salt
1/4 t. pepper

Melt butter in a large saucepan over medium heat. Add onion, mushrooms and rice; cook and stir for about 5 minutes, until rice is golden. Add remaining ingredients. Stir to dissolve gravy mix. Bring to a boil; reduce heat to low. Cover and cook for 20 to 25 minutes, until rice is tender and all liquid is absorbed. Makes 6 servings.

A quick fall craft...hot-glue large acorn caps onto
round magnets for whimsical fridge magnets.

Homestyle Creamed Corn

Lisa Langston
Montgomery, TX

This is simple and delicious...it tastes like home!

1/3 c. butter
1/3 c. all-purpose flour
1 c. whipping cream
1 c. milk
1/4 c. sugar

1/2 t. salt
1/2 t. pepper
5 c. corn, thawed if frozen
Optional: shredded Cheddar
cheese

Melt butter in a large saucepan over medium heat. Stir in flour until smooth. Gradually stir in cream, milk, sugar and seasonings. Bring to a low boil for 2 minutes, stirring constantly. Remove from heat; stir in corn. Transfer mixture to a lightly greased 1-1/2 quart casserole dish. Sprinkle cheese on top, if desired. Bake, uncovered, at 350 degrees for 10 to 15 minutes, until heated through. Makes 6 to 8 servings.

Thanksgiving dinner is all about tradition! Keep it simple with tried & true recipes everyone loves and anticipates like sweet potato casserole, corn pudding and cranberry sauce. If you like, add just one or two simple new dishes for variety. Then relax and enjoy your guests!

Buffet Potatoes

Ruth Ann Evans
Franklin Furnace, OH

*I got this recipe at the little country church that I attended.
It is very good. I make it for all the get-togethers and
it is everybody's favorite dish.*

32-oz. pkg. frozen hashbrown
    potatoes, thawed
1/2 c. onion, chopped
3/4 c. butter, melted and divided
10-3/4 oz. can cream of
    chicken soup
16-oz. container sour cream

1 t. salt
1/4 t. pepper
8-oz. pkg. shredded Cheddar
    cheese
1-1/2 c. corn flake cereal,
    crushed

In a large bowl, combine potatoes, onion and 1/2 cup melted butter.
Add soup, sour cream and seasonings; mix well. Fold in cheese;
transfer to a greased 13"x9" baking pan. In a small bowl, toss together
corn flakes and remaining melted butter; sprinkle over top. Bake,
uncovered, at 300 degrees for 1-1/2 hours. Serves 12.

Arrange baby veggies for dipping in a cornucopia basket!
Cherry tomatoes, snow peas, baby corn and mini mushrooms
are all pleasing to the eye and to the taste buds.

Grandma's Favorite Filling Balls
Kelly Thomas
Sarver, PA

This is the recipe I am asked to bring to every holiday function for family & friends alike. I use a loaf of store-brand bread and use a disposable foil pan to bake these in...no need to bring it home!

1/2 c. onion, chopped
1/2 c. celery, chopped
3/4 c. butter, melted and divided
20-oz. loaf sliced white
    bread, torn

14-3/4 oz. can creamed corn
3 eggs, lightly beaten
1/2 c. water
1/8 t. pepper

In a saucepan over medium heat, sauté onion and celery in 1/4 cup butter until tender. Remove from heat. In a large bowl, combine bread pieces, onion mixture, corn, eggs, water and pepper. Mix well; form into 12 to 14 balls, slightly smaller than a tennis ball. Arrange filling balls in a greased 13"x9" baking pan; balls should be touching. Drizzle with remaining melted butter. Bake, uncovered, at 350 degrees for 45 to 50 minutes, until golden. Makes 12 to 14 servings.

Save time by chopping lots of onion, celery, carrots and green pepper at once. Create your own sauté blend and freeze it in a freezer-safe container. Add it to skillet dishes straight from the freezer...there's no need to thaw!

Barley Pilaf

Vickie
Gooseberry Patch

A change from rice and potatoes! This savory side dish goes well with roast chicken or beef and goes together in a jiffy.

1 T. olive oil
1/2 c. onion, diced
1/2 c. carrot, peeled and diced
4-oz. can sliced mushrooms,
   drained

2 c. chicken or beef broth
1 c. quick-cooking barley,
   uncooked
1/4 t. salt
1/4 t. pepper

In a saucepan, heat oil over medium-high heat. Add vegetables. Cook, stirring occasionally, for 5 minutes. Add broth, barley and seasonings; stir well. Reduce heat to medium. Cover and simmer for 15 to 20 minutes, until tender, stirring occasionally. May add a little more broth or water if mixture becomes too dry. Serves 4.

Stock up on favorite pantry items like vegetables,
pasta and rice when they're on sale. They're so handy
for busy-day meals in a hurry.

FRESH-PICKED
Sides & Salads

Cauliflower Mash

Cindy McKinnon
El Dorado, AR

*I had no idea that cooking healthy whole foods could be
so much fun and taste so great! This is now a family favorite.*

1 head cauliflower, cut into
    flowerets
1/4 c. butter, sliced
1/4 c. sour cream

garlic powder, salt and pepper
    to taste
1/2 c. grated Parmesan cheese

In a saucepan, cover cauliflower with salted water. Bring to a boil;
cook until tender, about 10 minutes. Drain; cover and set aside for
10 minutes. (Do not omit this step.) Stir in butter, sour cream and
seasonings. Beat with an electric mixer on medium speed to desired
consistency. Stir in cheese. Makes 4 to 6 servings.

Beverly's Green Bean Casserole

Lesley Madosh
Shawano, WI

*My husband Shandy makes this for Thanksgiving every year. He
learned the recipe from his mother, who also made it for
Thanksgiving.*

1 lb. bacon
4 14-1/2 oz. cans cut green
    beans, drained
4-oz. can sliced mushrooms,
    drained

8-oz. pkg. shredded Cheddar
    cheese
1/2 t. garlic powder

Cook bacon in a skillet over medium heat until crisp. Remove bacon to
a paper towel; reserve drippings. Combine beans and mushrooms in a
lightly greased 13"x9" baking pan. Add crumbled bacon, cheese, garlic
powder and a little of reserved drippings. Mix gently. Bake, uncovered,
at 350 degrees for 30 minutes. Serves 8.

*An oh-so-simple harvest decoration...roll out a wheelbarrow
and heap it full of large, colorful squash and pumpkins.*

Johnny Appleseed Turkey Dressing

*Sue Webb
Casper, WY*

Back in 1975, as a newlywed with a hungry husband, this was the first stuffing I ever made. It's still deliciously different!

1/2 c. butter
1/2 c. onion, chopped
1 c. celery, chopped
2 tart apples, peeled, cored
 and chopped

2-1/2 c. chicken broth
14-oz. pkg. herb-seasoned
 stuffing cubes
4 slices bacon, crisply cooked
 and crumbled

Melt butter in a large skillet over medium heat. Add onion and celery; sauté until onion is transparent. Add apples and chicken broth; bring to a boil. Add stuffing cubes and bacon; mix well until moistened. Transfer dressing to a buttered 13"x9" baking pan. Cover and bake at 350 degrees for 35 to 45 minutes, until heated through. May also spoon dressing into an 8 to 10-pound turkey just before roasting; roast as desired. Serves 8 to 10.

Keep little ones busy and happy with a crafting area while the grown-ups put the finishing touches on Thanksgiving dinner. Set out paper plates to decorate with colored paper, feathers, pom-poms, crayons and washable glue. At dinnertime, they'll be proud to display their creations!

Pineapple-Glazed Carrots

Eleanor Dionne
Beverly, MA

We enjoy this dish year 'round. It's especially good when you have an abundance of carrots from the garden. The orange zest is a nice added touch.

5 to 7 carrots, peeled and cut
   into 1-1/2 inch sticks
1/2 t. salt
2 T. butter

1 c. pineapple tidbits, drained
1/2 c. light brown sugar, packed
1 T. orange zest
1/4 t. cinnamon

In a large saucepan, combine carrots with a small amount of water; add salt. Cook over medium heat until fork-tender; drain. Stir in remaining ingredients. Cook over medium heat for about 5 minutes, occasionally tossing lightly, until glazed. Serves 5 to 6.

∾∾

I grew up as a rice farmer's daughter, so autumn for me always brought the sights and sounds of combines in the rice fields and big trucks hauling the cut rice to the local rice dryer. I loved that time of year, as it meant I could ride with my dad on the combine harvester when he granted me the chance. He worked long, hard hours in the field getting the rice in, and it wasn't unusual to find him in the long line at the rice dryer after dark. One of my most special memories is getting off the school bus one afternoon and running into the house to find that my mother had fixed me a special treat as an after-school snack, a butterscotch sundae! As special as that was, I begged her to put it back in the freezer and take me over to the field where Dad was cutting rice so I could ride the combine. She just smiled, grabbed her car keys, told me to get in the car and said, "We will see." Dad saw us pull up and stopped the combine to see what she wanted. She told him, "Kay gave up a butterscotch sundae to come ride the combine!" Dad grinned, picked me up, walked across the field and helped me up into the seat of the combine. I felt like I was on top of the world!

–Kay Goings, Williford, AR

Favorite Spanish Rice

Hope Davenport
Portland, TX

I have tried many recipes for Spanish Rice over the years, and this is our favorite one. We love to eat cheese enchiladas and this flavorful rice, served with refried beans, rounds out a delicious meal.

1 c. long-cooking rice, uncooked
3/4 c. onion, chopped
1/2 green pepper, chopped
2 T. olive oil
2 c. chicken broth

10-oz. can diced tomatoes
  with green chiles
1/4 t. chili powder
salt to taste

In a skillet over medium heat, combine rice, onion, green pepper and oil. Cook over medium heat, stirring often, until onion is soft. Stir in chicken broth, tomatoes with juice and seasonings. Reduce heat to medium-low. Cover and simmer for about 20 minutes, until all liquid has been absorbed and rice is tender. Makes 4 servings.

Fill a muffin tin with fixings like shredded cheese, sliced black olives, chopped green onion and diced avocado. Everyone can top their own enchiladas or tacos to their liking.

Rancho Beans

Linda Garman
Caseville, MI

This recipe has been in our family for years. A family gathering is not complete without this dish...men really love it! Great as a side or even a main dish. It is quick, easy and delicious.

1 lb. ground beef
1/4 c. onion, chopped
1 T. mustard
1 T. Worcestershire sauce
28-oz. can pork & beans

15-1/2 oz. can kidney beans
1/2 c. brown sugar, packed
1/2 c. catsup
2 T. butter, diced

In a large skillet over medium heat, brown beef with onion; drain. Stir in mustard and Worcestershire sauce; heat through. In a large bowl, combine undrained beans, brown sugar and catsup; add to beef mixture and stir well. Transfer mixture to a lightly greased 2-quart casserole dish or bean pot. Dot with butter. Bake at 350 degrees for 30 to 40 minutes, stirring occasionally. Makes 6 servings.

There's a funny little fellow
Sitting out on our fence
And you know who I mean.
He came last night from Pumpkintown
To spend the Halloween.
–Old children's song

119

Yummy Good Tomato Crumble

Janis Parr
Ontario, Canada

This dish is so tasty and simple to make. I'm always asked
for the recipe whenever I take it to a potluck.

2 c. cabbage, shredded
3/4 c. cooked rice
2 c. canned diced tomatoes,
    drained
2 t. sugar
1/2 t. salt

1/8 t. pepper
1 c. dry bread crumbs
1 c. shredded Cheddar cheese
3 slices bacon, crisply cooked
    and crumbled
1 T. butter, diced

In a bowl, mix together cabbage, rice, tomatoes, sugar, salt and
pepper. Transfer to a greased 2-quart casserole dish. In a separate
bowl, combine bread crumbs, cheese and bacon; sprinkle over top of
tomato mixture. Dot with butter. Cover and bake at 350 degrees for
35 minutes, or until heated through. Serve hot. Makes 4 to 6 servings.

At autumn harvest, wrap any remaining green tomatoes in
newspaper and store in a warm spot. They'll slowly ripen
for you to enjoy later.

FRESH-PICKED
Sides & Salads

Sweet Potatoes with Cranberries

Cindy Masterson
Citrus Heights, CA

Even people who don't like cranberries come back for more! This is also delicious for dessert or warmed up for breakfast.

1 c. quick-cooking oats, uncooked
1 c. all-purpose flour
1 c. brown sugar, packed
2 t. cinnamon

1 c. butter, softened
2 29-oz. cans sweet potatoes, drained
4 c. fresh cranberries
3 c. mini marshmallows

Combine oats, flour, brown sugar, cinnamon and butter. Mix until crumbly; set aside. Add sweet potatoes to a separate large bowl; mix 2 cups of crumb mixture into yams. Add cranberries; mix well. Transfer to a lightly greased 13"x9" baking pan. Top with remaining crumb mixture. Bake, uncovered, at 350 degrees for about 45 minutes. Top with marshmallows; broil until melted, 2 to 4 minutes. Makes 12 to 14 servings.

Honey-Roasted Sweet Potatoes

Dale Duncan
Waterloo, IA

I first tried out this recipe as a lighter side for Thanksgiving. Now we enjoy it often with pork chops or fried chicken.

4 sweet potatoes, peeled and cut into 1-inch cubes
1/4 c. honey

5 T. olive oil, divided
2 t. cinnamon
salt and pepper to taste

Arrange sweet potatoes on a greased baking sheet in a single layer. Drizzle with honey and 4 tablespoons oil; sprinkle with seasonings. Bake at 375 degrees for 25 to 30 minutes, until tender. Transfer potatoes to a serving platter; drizzle with remaining oil. Serves 4.

We all have hometown appetites.
–Clementine Paddleford

121

Homemade Spiced Applesauce

Lori Ritchey
Denver, PA

After I started making this recipe I realized that I did not have a lemon on hand. So I improvised and used an orange instead...a whoops became a wow! It turned out even better. This also works well as pie filling.

3 lbs. assorted Gala, Granny
   Smith and Red Delicious
   apples, peeled, cored and
   quartered
1 c. light brown sugar, packed
1/2 c. water

juice of 1/4 orange or
   1/2 lemon
1/4 t. cinnamon
1/8 t. nutmeg
1 T. butter, sliced

Combine all ingredients in a large saucepan over medium heat. Simmer, uncovered until very soft, stirring often, about 15 to 20 minutes. Serve hot or chilled. Makes 6 servings.

Add rosy red color and spicy flavor to homemade
applesauce! Just stir in a spoonful of red cinnamon
candies as it's cooking.

FRESH-PICKED
Sides & Salads

Super-Simple Cranberry Sauce

Jen Jennings
Richmond, VA

The battle has been going on for years...canned or homemade? One Thanksgiving, after a hectic holiday morning, my mother suggested we just have canned cranberry sauce, as it was quicker. Instead, I pulled out this little trick! I had my cranberry sauce made and in the dish before she could locate her special cranberry serving dish, turn it out of the can (in one piece!) and onto the dish.

12-oz. pkg. fresh cranberries
1 T. orange zest

1 c. sugar
1/2 c. water

Combine all ingredients in a microwave-safe bowl. Cover with plastic wrap. Microwave on high until the cranberries pop, about 7 minutes. Serve warm, or chill before serving. Serves 6.

There's always room for one more at the harvest table. Why not invite a neighbor or a college student who might be spending the holiday alone to share your Thanksgiving feast?

Cranberry-Wild Rice Salad

Marcia Marcoux
Charlton, MA

This salad has it all...tender wild rice, tangy cranberries and orange zest, the crunch of pine nuts and the taste of fresh parsley. Perfect for fall, and it feeds a crowd!

6-1/2 c. water
1/2 c. chicken broth
2-1/2 c. wild rice, uncooked
1 c. sweetened dried cranberries
1 c. golden raisins
1 c. green onions, chopped
3/4 c. pine nuts, toasted

1/2 c. fresh parsley, chopped
2 T. orange zest
1/2 c. orange juice
1/4 c. cider vinegar
1/2 c. olive oil
salt and pepper to taste

Bring water and broth to a boil in a large saucepan over high heat. Add rice; reduce heat to medium. Cover and simmer until rice is cooked yet slightly firm, about 40 minutes, stirring occasionally. Drain; transfer rice to a large bowl to cool. Add cranberries, raisins, onions, pine nuts, parsley and orange zest; toss to mix and set aside. In a small bowl, whisk together orange juice and vinegar. Slowly whisk in oil. Drizzle dressing over rice; toss to coat. Season with salt and pepper. Cover and refrigerate for 2 to 3 hours. Bring to room temperature before serving. Makes 10 to 12 servings.

If you love fresh cranberries, stock up when they're available in the fall. Pop unopened bags in the freezer...you'll be able to add their fruity tang to recipes year 'round.

FRESH-PICKED
Sides & Salads

Glazed Fruit Salad

Linda Barker
Mount Pleasant, TN

This recipe was given to me years ago by a lady who always brought it to our church dinners. It's delicious...she always went home with an empty bowl!

15-oz. can fruit cocktail, drained
11-oz. can mandarin oranges,
    drained
15-1/4 oz. can pineapple
    chunks, drained

21-oz. can peach pie filling
2 bananas, sliced
1 c. flaked coconut
1 c. mini marshmallows
Optional: 3/4 c. chopped pecans

In a serving bowl, combine all ingredients. Gently stir to mix well. Cover and refrigerate at least 2 hours before serving. Serves 6.

Easy Apple-Nut Slaw

Carolyn Deckard
Bedford, IN

This is the easiest way to make slaw when you are in a hurry. Sometimes I buy shredded slaw mix to save even more time.

3 c. green cabbage, shredded
1 c. red cabbage, shredded
2 red apples, cored and sliced

1 c. chopped walnuts, toasted
1-1/2 c. regular or low-fat ranch
    salad dressing

Combine all ingredients in a large bowl; toss gently to coat. Cover and refrigerate until ready to serve. Makes 4 to 6 servings.

Toast nuts for extra flavor! Place walnuts or pecans in a skillet in a single layer. Shake over medium-high heat continually for 5 to 7 minutes, until the nuts turn golden and toasty smelling.

Broccoli Salad with Poppy Seed Dressing

Debra King
Gilbertville, MA

Combining ingredients ahead always adds to the flavor. Just keep the salad and dressing separate till just before serving time.

8 to 10 slices bacon, crisply
    cooked and crumbled
1 c. raisins

1 bunch broccoli, cut into
    bite-size flowerets
1/2 c. red onion, chopped

Combine all ingredients in a large bowl; toss to mix. Just before serving, spoon Poppy Seed Dressing over salad; toss again. Makes 8 servings.

Poppy Seed Dressing:

1 c. mayonnaise
1/3 c. sugar

1/3 c. red wine vinegar
1 T. poppy seed

Combine all ingredients; whisk together well.

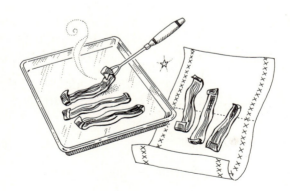

Crispy bacon the easy way...bake it. Place bacon slices on a broiler pan, place the pan in the oven and turn the temperature to 400 degrees. Bake for 12 to 15 minutes, turn bacon over and bake for another 8 to 10 minutes. No fuss, no grease spatters on the stovetop!

All-American Potato Salad

Mary Muchowicz
Elk Grove Village, IL

I love this potato salad because it is made with new redskin potatoes and red pepper, celery and onion give it a lot of crunch. The dressing really finishes it off well. Excellent with burgers, chicken, brats and other cookout food...perfect for tailgating!

3 qts. water
3 lbs. new redskin potatoes,
    cut in half
3/4 c. mayonnaise
1 T. cider vinegar
2 t. light cream
2 t. Dijon mustard

1 T. sugar
1 t. salt
1/8 t. pepper
1 c. onion, minced
1 red pepper, cut into
    1/4-inch-thick strips
1 stalk celery, thinly sliced

Bring water to a boil in a stockpot over high heat. Add potatoes. Cook for 12 minutes, or until potatoes are easily pierced with a fork. Drain; set pot with potatoes in a large bowl of ice water to stop cooking. When potatoes are cool, transfer to a colander; set aside until well drained. In a large bowl, combine mayonnaise, vinegar, cream, mustard, sugar, salt and pepper. Add potatoes, onion, red pepper and celery; toss gently to coat. Cover with plastic wrap; refrigerate at least one hour to blend ingredients. Makes 8 to 10 servings.

ooompah!

Throw an Oktoberfest party for family & friends! Set a festive mood with polka music. Toss some brats on the grill to serve in hard rolls...don't forget the spicy mustard! Round out the menu with potato salad, homemade applesauce and German chocolate cake for dessert.

Baby Spinach Salad with Avocado

Sonya Labbe
West Hollywood, CA

I love to serve this salad during the holiday season. It is beautiful and so good. Company always loves it!

2 5-oz. pkgs. baby spinach
2 Granny Smith apples, peeled,
   cored and diced
2 ripe avocados, pitted and
   coarsely chopped

6-oz. pkg. crumbled blue cheese
1 c. pecan halves, toasted
1/2 c. dried cranberries

In a large bowl, combine all ingredients; toss to mix. Lightly drizzle salad with desired amount of Honey-Orange Dressing; toss gently to coat. Serves 6.

Honey-Orange Dressing:

3 T. cider vinegar
2 T. orange juice
2 T. honey

2-1/2 t. Dijon mustard
2/3 c. extra virgin olive oil
salt and pepper to taste

Whisk together vinegar, orange juice, honey and mustard. Slowly whisk in oil in a steady stream. Season with salt and pepper.

Keep salad greens farmstand-fresh for up to a week. After you bring them home, rinse greens in cool water, wrap in paper towels and slip into a plastic zipping bag with several small holes cut in it. Tuck the bag in the fridge's crisper bin...ready to serve when you are!

Roasted Potato Salad

Diane Cohen
Breinigsville, PA

This salad is delicious warm or chilled.

2-1/2 to 3 lbs. Yukon Gold or
   russet potatoes, cut into
   1-inch cubes
3/4 c. onion, chopped
4 cloves garlic, coarsely chopped
2 T. olive oil

8 slices bacon, chopped
1/2 c. mayonnaise
1/2 c. sour cream
1/4 c. fresh parsley, chopped
2 T. white balsamic vinegar
1/4 c. pepper

In a large bowl, combine potatoes, onion, garlic and olive oil; toss to mix. Spread on a lightly oiled baking sheet in a single layer. Bake at 400 degrees for 30 minutes, tossing after 15 minutes. Set aside to cool. Place bacon in a large microwave-safe bowl, separating pieces; place a paper towel on top. Microwave on high for 9 to 12 minutes, stirring every 3 minutes, until crisp and golden. Remove bacon with a slotted spoon; drain on paper towels. In a small bowl, combine remaining ingredients; blend well. Combine potato mixture with bacon and mayonnaise mixture in a serving bowl; toss to coat. Serve slightly warm, or cover and chill. Makes 8 servings.

Share the warmth. With winter on the way, autumn is
a perfect time to pull outgrown coats, hats and mittens
out of closets and donate them to a local charity.

Mexican Slaw

Ashley Jones
Gates, NC

*This recipe was handed down to my mom by her mom. We make it
every Sunday and the bowl gets filled up three times...it goes fast. It's
such a good Sunday dish! Enjoy as a side salad, as an appetizer with
tortilla chips or spooned over a Mexican-style main dish.*

1 head cabbage, shredded
1 c. grape tomatoes, sliced
1/2 c. white onion, coarsely
    chopped
1/2 c. red onion, coarsely
    chopped
2 green onions, finely chopped
2 bunches fresh cilantro,
    coarsely chopped

2 4-oz. cans chopped jalapeño
    peppers
1/4 c. olive oil
3 T. rice vinegar
1 t. garlic powder
2 t. ground cumin
salt and pepper to taste

Toss together fresh vegetables and cilantro in a large bowl. Add
jalapeños with juice and remaining ingredients; toss again. Let stand
30 minutes before serving. Makes 12 to 14 servings.

Packing for a picnic or potluck? Keep food in coolers fresh with
homemade ice packs. In a gallon-size plastic zipping bag, combine
2 cups water, one cup rubbing alcohol and 2 to 3 drops blue food
coloring. Seal very well, leaving room for expansion, and freeze.
Refreeze and re-use bags several times.

FRESH-PICKED
Sides & Salads

Corn Chip Salad to Go

Michelle Powell
Valley, AL

Perfect tailgate food! Just mix the salad and serve in individual corn chip bags.

1 to 2 ripe tomatoes, chopped
1 head iceberg lettuce, chopped
1 onion, chopped
16-oz. pkg. shredded Cheddar cheese
15-oz. can ranch-style beans, drained
8-oz. bottle Catalina salad dressing
6 2-oz. pkgs. corn chips

In a large bowl, combine all ingredients except corn chips. Toss to mix; let stand for one hour. At serving time, slit open corn chip bags down one side. Spoon salad over corn chips in bags and serve immediately. Serves 6.

Growing up in Ohio, I enjoyed my life every fall, playing in the apple orchard, raking up leaves, getting ready for Halloween, and then, wow, Thanksgiving! While my two children were growing up, I made sure that they had memories of this exciting time of the year too. Now that I am a grandparent, it is awesome! We would go to Neumeier Nursery in Fort Smith, Arkansas in mid-October for their Pumpkin Patch Fall Festival. It is wonderful. Vendors from all over bring crafts and baked goods, and of course there is live music. My daughter and stepdaughter bring the grandbabies so we can let the kids pick out what they want. So much fun to see the kids' excited faces, trying to carry these large pumpkins, as if they can carry the world. And of course, this Gramms is snapping away with my camera. We'd laugh and have such a wonderful time every year. I have moved away now, but I try my best to make it back every fall. If I can't, I know my girls will take pictures of all the fun for me.

–Loraine Briggs, Fort Smith, AR

Festive Tossed Salad

*Betty Block
Kendall, MI*

With cranberries, apple and pear, this salad is perfect for autumn. I like to use powdered sweetener in the dressing.

10 c. romaine lettuce, torn
1 red apple, cored and chopped
1 firm pear, cored and chopped
1 c. shredded Swiss cheese

1/4 c. sweetened dried
   cranberries
1/2 to 1 c. cashew halves

In a salad bowl, combine all ingredients except cashews. Drizzle with desired amount of Poppy Seed-Red Wine Dressing. Add cashews; toss to coat. Serve immediately. Makes 8 to 10 servings.

Poppy Seed-Red Wine Dressing:

1/2 c. sugar
1/3 c. red wine vinegar
2 T. lemon juice
2 T. onion, finely chopped

1/2 t. salt
2/3 c. oil
2 to 3 t. poppy seed

In a blender, combine sugar, vinegar, lemon juice, onion and salt. Cover and process until blended. With blender running, gradually add oil. Add poppy seed and blend.

Head out to a pick-your-own apple orchard for a day of fresh-air fun. The kids will love it, and you'll come home with bushels of the best-tasting apples for applesauce, cobblers and crisps.

Apple, Nut & Celery Salad

Audra LeNormand
Liberty, TX

Our family has served this salad every Thanksgiving and Christmas for as long as I can remember. My Great-Grandma Biggs, my MawMaw, Mom and now me. It's easy to fix and really good!

3 red apples, cored and chopped
6 stalks celery, finely chopped
juice of 1 lemon
1 c. chopped pecans

Optional: 1 c. seedless grapes, halved
1 c. mayonnaise-type salad dressing

Combine apples and celery in a salad bowl; drizzle with lemon juice. Add pecans and mix again; stir in salad dressing. If mixture seems a bit dry, add a little more salad dressing. Serves 6.

Pauline's 1-2-3 Coleslaw

Pauline Banks
Austin, TX

My husband's favorite coleslaw. It's a little more on the sweet side rather than the traditional tangy side.

12-oz. pkg. shredded
   coleslaw mix
8-oz. can crushed pineapple

1/2 c. mayonnaise-type
   salad dressing

Combine coleslaw mix, pineapple with juice and salad dressing. Toss to mix thoroughly. Add more salad dressing, if desired. Cover and chill until serving time. Makes 6 servings.

Make a chopped salad in seconds... no cutting board needed! Add greens and veggies to a big bowl, then roll a pizza cutter back & forth over them. Drizzle with dressing and enjoy your salad.

Holiday Cranberry Salad

Arlinda Bui
Saint Petersburg, FL

This was a favorite holiday recipe in my family, especially with Thanksgiving turkey dinner. It makes enough for the whole family!

3-oz. pkg. strawberry or
   raspberry gelatin mix
3/4 c. boiling water
15-oz. can whole-berry
   cranberry sauce

1 red apple, peeled, cored
   and chopped
1/2 c. celery, chopped
1/2 c. chopped walnuts

In a large bowl, combine gelatin mix and boiling water. Stir until gelatin is dissolved. Add cranberry sauce, breaking up with a spoon; mix until smooth. Stir in apple, celery and nuts. Cover and chill until set. Makes 15 servings.

Let everyone know what's inside each dish at the next buffet or potluck. Write each dish's name on a beautiful real or faux autumn leaf using a gold or silver metallic marker.

DOWN-HOME
Dinners to Share

Shortcut Lasagna

Judith Biggs
Coquille, OR

I have a great recipe for traditional lasagna, but one night when we were expecting our grandchildren for dinner, I needed something quick and kid-friendly. I came up with this, hoping it would be easier on the little ones' more sensitive taste buds. I paired this with warm crusty bread and a simple green salad...they loved it!

2-1/2 c. elbow macaroni,
   uncooked
1 lb. lean ground beef
26-oz. jar 4-cheese pasta sauce
6-oz. can sliced black olives,
   drained
1/4 c. grated Parmesan cheese

16-oz. container low-fat
   cottage cheese
2 eggs, beaten
1/2 t. dried basil
1-1/2 c. shredded mozzarella
   cheese, divided

Cook macaroni according to package directions; drain and return to pot. Meanwhile, brown beef in a skillet over medium heat; drain. Stir pasta sauce and olives into beef; add to macaroni and combine thoroughly. In a small bowl, whisk together Parmesan and cottage cheeses, eggs and basil. Spread half of macaroni mixture evenly in a 13"x9" baking pan coated with non-stick vegetable spray; sprinkle with 3/4 cup mozzarella cheese. Spread cottage cheese mixture evenly over cheese. Carefully add remaining macaroni mixture; spread evenly. Top with remaining cheese. Bake, uncovered, at 350 degrees for 30 minutes. Cut into squares. Makes 8 servings.

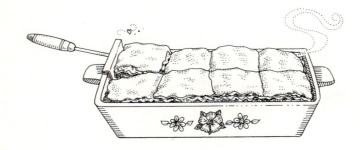

Let the kids invite a special friend or two home for dinner. Keep it simple with a hearty casserole and a relish tray of crunchy veggies & dip. A great way to get to know your children's school friends!

Smoked Sausage Penne

Liz Brooks
Lexington, KY

My family loves this pasta dish because of the
hint of spice, especially on cold nights!

8-oz. pkg. penne pasta,
  uncooked
1 crown broccoli, chopped
1 lb. smoked pork sausage
  link, cubed

1 T. all-purpose flour
2 c. whipping cream
2 t. smoked seasoning blend
1/2 c. shredded Parmesan
  cheese, divided

Cook pasta according to package directions. Add broccoli to pot during the last 4 minutes of cooking time; drain. Meanwhile, in a skillet over medium heat, cook sausage for 5 minutes. Sprinkle flour over sausage; toss to coat. Add cream and seasoning; simmer over medium-low heat until thickened. Stir in 1/4 cup Parmesan cheese. Add sausage mixture to pasta mixture; toss to coat well. Sprinkle with remaining cheese and serve immediately. Serves 5.

Give favorite pasta recipes a twist for fall...pick up some pasta in seasonal shapes like autumn leaves, pumpkins or turkeys! Some even come in veggie colors like orange, red and green.

Chicken & Potato Bake

Rebecca Etling
Blairsville, PA

One of my favorite quick comfort meals.

2 c. boiling water
4 cubes chicken bouillon
32-oz. pkg. frozen diced
    potatoes, thawed
1 c. garlic croutons, crushed
1 t. salt
1/2 t. pepper
4 c. cooked chicken, cubed
4-oz. can mushroom stems &
    pieces, drained

8-oz. container sour cream
10-3/4 oz. can cream of chicken
    soup
2 T. onion, chopped
2 t. garlic powder
1 to 2 t. paprika
3/4 c. shredded sharp Cheddar
    cheese

Combine boiling water and bouillon cubes; set aside. Spread potatoes in a greased 13"x9" baking pan. Mix in crushed croutons; sprinkle with salt and pepper. Spread chicken and mushrooms over top; set aside. In a bowl, combine sour cream, soup, bouillon mixture, onion and garlic powder; mix well and spoon over top. Sprinkle with paprika. Bake, uncovered, at 350 degrees for 50 to 60 minutes, until hot and bubbly. Top with cheese; let stand until melted. Serves 8 to 10.

On busy fall weekends, a simple make-ahead casserole is perfect. Assemble it the night before and refrigerate, then pop it in the oven when you return from barn sale-ing, leaf peeping or getting an early start on holiday shopping.

Kielbasa & Cabbage Skillet

Diana Robbins
Flat Rock, MI

In just a few minutes, you can put a hearty meal on the table! Add chopped green pepper or a small drained can of corn, if you like.

2 T. butter
1-lb. Kielbasa sausage link,
    cut into one-inch slices
1 red onion, sliced
16-oz. pkg. shredded coleslaw
    mix

1/2 c. chicken broth
1 t. garlic powder
salt to taste
1/2 t. pepper

Melt butter in a large skillet over medium heat. Add sausage and onion; sauté until onion is tender. Add remaining ingredients to skillet. Cook and stir for 8 to 10 minutes, until heated through. Serves 4.

Smoked sausage is a great choice for fast-fix meals...just heat and serve. Different flavors like hickory-smoked or cheese-filled sausage can really jazz up a recipe, or try smoked turkey sausage for a lean and healthy alternative.

Parmesan Chicken Strips

Bootsie Dominick
Sandy Springs, GA

*So simple! This chicken is good with seasoned rice
or cut into pieces and served over a tossed salad.*

1/2 c. butter, melted
1 c. dry bread crumbs
1/2 c. grated Parmesan cheese
1/4 c. fresh parsley, minced
2 t. garlic salt

1/8 t. pepper
4 boneless, skinless chicken
   breasts, halved lengthwise
   and cut into strips

Place melted butter in a shallow dish; set aside. Combine bread crumbs, cheese, parsley and seasonings in a large plastic zipping bag; shake to mix. Dip chicken strips into butter; add to crumb mixture and shake to coat well. Arrange strips on an ungreased rimmed baking sheet. Bake at 350 degrees for one hour, or until golden and chicken juices run clear. Serves 4 to 6.

Tasty Chicken Nuggets

Stephanie D'Esposito
Ravena, NY

*My three daughters request these tasty nuggets at least twice
a week. They are a quick & easy alternative to frozen nuggets.*

1 egg, beaten
1 c. ranch salad dressing
2 c. seasoned dry bread crumbs

1 lb. boneless, skinless chicken
   breasts, cut into nugget-size
   cubes

Mix egg and salad dressing in a shallow dish; set aside. Add bread crumbs to another shallow dish. Dip chicken into egg mixture, then into crumb mixture. Place nuggets on a greased baking sheet. Bake at 375 degrees for 30 minutes, turning after 15 minutes, until nuggets are crisp and golden on both sides. Makes 4 servings.

Whip up a yummy Parmesan dip for French fries. Combine 1/2 cup mayonnaise, 1/4 cup grated Parmesan cheese and 1/4 teaspoon garlic powder. Chill until serving time.

Creamy Salsa Chicken Tenders

*Jo Ann
Gooseberry Patch*

This dish is really quick and delicious. We enjoy it with a chopped salad of lettuce, tomato and avocado...dinner in a dash!

3 lbs. boneless chicken tenders
Creole seasoning, salt and
    pepper to taste
1/4 c. olive oil

2 c. chunky salsa
1/2 c. sour cream
cooked rice

Sprinkle chicken with seasonings. Heat olive oil in a large skillet over medium heat. Add chicken and cook until golden, about 3 minutes per side. Remove chicken to a plate. Pour salsa into pan; cook and stir for 2 minutes. Reduce heat to low; stir in sour cream. Return chicken to pan and turn to coat. Cover and simmer for 4 to 5 minutes. Serve chicken and sauce over cooked rice. Serves 6.

We always went to my Aunt Sarah & Uncle Sam's house for Thanksgiving. The day would start early and the autumn air was crisp. While the "boys" (my two sons, a brother and a cousin) left early to go deer hunting, the "girls" (my aunt, my cousin, my mother & me) cooked the Thanksgiving dinner. Our dinner was a dish of ground beef & beans we called "Haystacks." Aunt Sarah always made that for my boys because they loved it so much. She also cooked traditional foods like dressing, sweet potatoes, corn and peas. At dinnertime, Aunt Sarah would walk out to the backyard and ring the big black bell three times to call in the guys from the woods. As they washed up, you could hear them talking excitedly about the deer they had seen and how it got away. Then we all sat down to eat our dinner and enjoy the togetherness we shared. We still look forward to this Thanksgiving tradition. My Aunt Sarah, who started this tradition, is no longer with us, but the tradition will carry on.

–April Smith, Jemison, AL

Easy Hungarian Goulash

Kathy Courington
Canton, GA

My mother made meals like this for us when I was growing up.
This recipe still reminds me of home, coming in after school
and smelling it from kitchen. Wonderful memories!

2 lbs. beef round steak, cut into
    1/2-inch cubes
2 T. all-purpose flour
1 to 2 t. paprika
1/8 t. dried thyme
3/4 t. salt
1/4 t. pepper

15-1/2 oz. can diced tomatoes
1 c. onion, chopped
1 clove garlic, minced
1 bay leaf
8-oz. container sour cream
cooked wide egg noodles

Add beef cubes to a 4-quart slow cooker; set aside. Combine flour and
seasonings; sprinkle over beef and mix well to coat. Add tomatoes
with juice, onion and garlic. Cover and cook on low setting for 8 to
10 hours. About 30 minutes before cooking time is done, stir in sour
cream. Cover and finish cooking. If preferred, sour cream may be
served on the side. At serving time, discard bay leaf. Ladle beef
mixture over cooked noodles. Serves 4 to 6.

A family recipe book is a wonderful way to preserve
one generation's traditions for the next. Ask everyone to send
copies of their most-requested recipes, and combine all the
recipes into a book. Have enough copies made for everyone...
a delightful take-home for Thanksgiving dinner.

Pasta Fagioli

Kathy Collins
Brookfield, CT

My family loves it when I make this dish. It's thicker than a soup...great for those cold, damp rainy days of autumn.

5 T. olive oil
1 yellow onion, chopped
3 cloves garlic, chopped
3-1/2 c. water
26-oz. jar marinara sauce
3 carrots, peeled and chopped
4 stalks celery, chopped
19-oz. can cannellini beans, drained and rinsed

3 cubes chicken bouillon
1/2 t. dried basil
1/2 t. red pepper flakes
16-oz. pkg. ditalini pasta, uncooked
Garnish: grated Parmesan cheese

Add olive oil to a stockpot over medium-high heat. Add onion and garlic; cook until golden and caramelized, 10 to 15 minutes. Add remaining ingredients except pasta and garnish. Reduce heat to medium; cover loosely. Simmer for about 35 minutes, stirring every 10 to 15 minutes, until sauce is thickened. Meanwhile, cook pasta according to package directions. Drain pasta and add to sauce; stir until pasta is well coated. Top with Parmesan cheese at serving time. Makes 4 to 6 servings.

To remove the smell of garlic from your hands, simply rub your hands with a stainless steel spoon or other utensil while holding them under cold running water.

Double-Stuffed Barbecue Potatoes

Tina Goodpasture
Meadowview, VA

If you like barbecue, you'll love these hearty stuffed potatoes...
they're a meal in one. I love potatoes any way I can find to fix them!

8 baking potatoes
8-oz. pkg. cream cheese,
  softened
1/2 c. mayonnaise
1 T. white wine vinegar
2 t. lemon juice

3/4 t. salt
1 t. seasoned pepper
3 c. barbecue pork, chopped
  and warmed
1 c. shredded Cheddar cheese
1/4 c. fresh chives, chopped

Wrap each potato in a piece of aluminum foil; place potatoes on a baking sheet. Bake at 425 degrees for 45 minutes, or until fork-tender. Cut a 4-inch by 2-inch strip from the top of each baked potato. Carefully scoop out potato pulp into a large bowl, leaving potato shells intact. Set aside 2 cups of pulp for another use. Combine remaining pulp, cream cheese, mayonnaise, vinegar, lemon juice and seasonings. Mash together with a fork; stir in pork. Spoon mixture evenly into potato shells; top evenly with Cheddar cheese and chives. Place on a lightly greased baking sheet. Bake at 375 degrees for 20 to 25 minutes, until heated through and cheese is melted. Serves 8.

On brisk harvest nights, sitting around a bonfire is oh-so cozy.
And you can cook the same family-favorite recipes over a
campfire that you can cook on a gas or charcoal grill...
hot dogs, steaks, hamburgers, chicken, even shish kabobs!

Dinners to Share

BBQ Chicken Flatbread

Jennifer Rubino
Hickory, NC

The flavor of barbecue chicken reminds me of campfires and smoke pits. Serve sliced apples with a caramel dipping sauce for dessert, and you've got all the flavors of fall. Happy fall, y'all!

4 flatbreads
6 T. barbecue sauce
24 slices deli oven-roasted
    chicken

1 c. shredded Cheddar cheese

Place each flatbread on a piece of foil; arrange on baking sheets. Spread each flatbread with 1-1/2 tablespoons barbecue sauce; layer with 6 slices of chicken. Sprinkle cheese over all. Bake at 350 degrees for 5 minutes, or until cheese is melted. Makes 4 servings.

BBQ Pork Pizza

Courtney Stultz
Weir, KS

This is one of those "toss-together-leftover" meals that is so good I have to share. We had a lot of leftover smoked pork after an event, and this pizza was the perfect way to make use of all of it. The green peppers really complement the BBQ sauce too.

1 prebaked Italian pizza crust
1/4 c. barbecue sauce
2 c. barbecue pulled pork

1/2 c. green pepper, diced
1/4 c. onion, diced
1 c. shredded pizza-blend cheese

Place pizza crust on a baking sheet. Spread with barbecue sauce. Top with pork, green pepper and onion; sprinkle with cheese. Bake at 425 degrees for 12 to 15 minutes, until hot and cheese is melted. Cool for 10 minutes; cut into wedges. Makes 6 servings.

It's fun to get together and have something good to eat at least once a day. That's what human life is all about...enjoying things.
–Julia Child

Pork Chops with Apples & Sweet Potatoes

Debra Stephens
Owasso, OK

*One night I was looking for a way to use up
extra apples and sweet potatoes...and voilà!*

1 c. all-purpose flour
1 t. onion powder
1 t. seasoned salt
1/2 t. pepper
6 thick boneless or bone-in
    pork chops
2 to 3 sweet potatoes, peeled
    and cubed

2 to 3 Granny Smith apples,
    cored and sliced or cubed
1/2 c. brown sugar, packed
1 t. cinnamon
Optional: 1/8 t. pumpkin pie
    spice
1 to 2 T. olive oil

In a shallow dish, combine flour, onion powder, seasoned salt and
pepper. Lightly coat pork chops with flour mixture; reserve remaining
flour mixture. Spray a rimmed baking sheet with non-stick vegetable
spray. Arrange pork chops on pan, leaving some space between pork
chops; set aside. In a bowl, combine remaining ingredients and a few
tablespoons of reserved flour mixture. Thoroughly mix to coat.
Arrange sweet potatoes and apples on pan between the pork chops.
Drizzle with olive oil. Bake at 350 degrees for one hour, or until pork
chops are golden and sweet potatoes are tender. Serves 6.

Press whole cloves into the surface of a gold or orange pillar
candle to form a pattern...just right for a harvest table.

Papa's Favorite Baked Dijon Pork Chops

Marge Smith
Tulsa, OK

My sweet husband just loves these pork chops...it's the only way he eats them! It's a simple, quickly put together meal that satisfies everyone...from a big man's appetite clear down to our 5-year-old granddaughter, who loves them too! I serve with baked potatoes and in summer months, fresh corn on the cob tops it off perfectly. Looks like a meal that took all day to put together, but it's not!

1/4 c. Dijon mustard
1/4 c. Italian salad dressing
4 boneless pork chops

1/2 onion, sliced and separated
  into rings

Mix together mustard and salad dressing. Pour a small amount onto a parchment paper-lined baking sheet, spreading it around. Arrange pork chops over mustard mixture on baking sheet. Layer sliced onion on the top of each pork chop. Drizzle remaining mustard mixture over all. Bake at 400 degrees for 40 minutes, or until pork chops are tender and golden. Makes 4 servings.

Sometimes the simplest front door decorations are the prettiest! Gather 5 or 6 brightly colored ears of Indian corn by the dried husks and tie with a big ribbon bow.

Dad's Potato Tot Casserole

Helen McKay
Edmond, OK

This is an easy meal to make. After Mom passed away, whenever we went to visit Dad, he always made this casserole for us. Our families loved it, especially the grandkids. He was happy when we asked for this recipe to share with our families.

1 lb. ground beef
2 10-3/4 oz. cans cream of
    mushroom soup
1 c. whole milk

5-oz. can evaporated milk
32-oz. pkg. frozen potato puffs
12-oz. pkg. shredded Cheddar
    cheese

Brown beef in a large skillet over medium heat. Drain; stir in soup and milks. Add potato puffs and cheese; stir gently to coat. Transfer to a greased 13"x9" baking pan. Bake, uncovered, at 350 degrees for one hour. Serves 8.

Saucy Short Ribs & Potatoes

Patricia Nau
River Grove, IL

One of my mom's recipes...easy, but so good! You'll love the aroma as it bakes all afternoon.

3 lbs. beef short ribs
1/4 c. French salad dressing
2 yellow onions, thinly sliced

3 c. beef broth or water
8 new potatoes, halved

Brush short ribs with salad dressing; let stand for one hour. Spray a 13"x9" baking pan with non-stick vegetable spray. Arrange short ribs in pan; arrange onion slices on top. Pour broth around beef. Cover and bake at 350 degrees for one hour. Add potatoes to pan; cover again and bake one hour longer, or until tender. Uncover; bake 30 minutes more. Makes 6 servings.

Share family stories behind the special dishes that are a tradition at every holiday dinner.

DOWN-HOME
Dinners to Share

Grandma's Hamburger Hotdish
Shana Anspach
Montevideo, MN

*This is one of our family favorites. My grandma made this for years,
and now I make it for mine. I love it because it is quick and simple,
yet full of flavor. Serve with warm garlic toast...delicious.*

16-oz. pkg. wide egg egg
   noodles, uncooked
1 lb. ground beef
10-3/4 oz. can tomato soup

2 c. favorite pasta sauce
16-oz. can kidney beans,
   drained
1/4 c. butter, sliced

Cook noodles according to package directions; drain. Meanwhile,
brown beef in a skillet over medium heat; drain. Stir soup and sauce
into beef. Add beef mixture and beans to cooked noodles; mix well.
Transfer to a greased 3-quart casserole dish and dot with butter. Cover
and bake at 350 degrees for 25 to 30 minutes, until hot and bubbly.
Makes 6 to 8 servings.

Write a sweet word of thanks or a harvest quote on strips
of paper and fasten to the outside of glasses with double-sided
tape. When Thanksgiving guests are seated, invite everyone
to read their quote aloud.

Mary's Chicken & Artichoke Dinner

Mary Plut
Hackettstown, NJ

A co-worker shared this speedy skillet recipe with me, and I make it often. I never used to eat artichokes, but the marinade from the artichokes makes such a tasty sauce, my family doesn't groan when they hear we're having chicken for dinner!

1 egg
1 c. Italian-flavored dry bread
   crumbs
4 boneless, skinless chicken
   breasts
2 T. olive oil

12-oz. jar marinated artichoke
   hearts, drained and liquid
   reserved
2 tomatoes, chopped
Optional: cooked rice or pasta

Beat egg in a shallow bowl; add bread crumbs to another shallow bowl. Dip chicken into egg, then into bread crumbs; set aside. Heat oil in a skillet over medium heat. Add chicken; cook on both sides until golden and juices no longer run pink. Add reserved artichoke liquid to skillet. Reduce heat to low and simmer for 5 to 7 minutes, stirring occasionally. Add artichokes and tomatoes; cook another 10 minutes. To serve, remove chicken to 4 dinner plates, with cooked rice or pasta if desired. Top with artichokes, tomatoes and sauce from skillet. Makes 4 servings.

Use chalk to write a seasonal message on a small chalkboard in your prettiest script...a heartfelt greeting to guests!

Easy Turkey Manicotti

Katie Brumm
Osage, IA

My husband's absolute favorite...and you don't even
have to cook the manicotti shells separately!

1 lb. ground turkey
salt and pepper to taste
1 T. Italian seasoning
16-oz. container cottage cheese

12 manicotti shells, uncooked
26-oz. jar pasta sauce
8-oz. pkg. shredded mozzarella
cheese

Brown turkey in a skillet over medium heat; drain and sprinkle with seasonings. Remove from heat; stir in cottage cheese and a little more Italian seasoning, if desired. Spoon mixture into uncooked manicotti shells. Arrange stuffed shells in a greased 13"x9" baking pan. Spoon pasta sauce over shells. Cover with aluminum foil. Bake at 350 degrees for 50 minutes. Top with mozzarella cheese. Bake, uncovered, for 5 minutes, or until cheese is melted. Let stand for a few minutes before serving. Serves 6.

If you're traveling to join family for Thanksgiving, make a trip bag for each of the kids...a special tote bag that's filled with favorite small toys, puzzles and other fun stuff reserved just for road trips. The miles will speed by much faster!

Best Thanksgiving Turkey

Liz Blackstone
Racine, WI

*You'll feel like a champ on Thanksgiving when you take
this delicious turkey to the dinner table! It's really not
that difficult when you use this recipe.*

10 to 12-pound turkey, thawed
   if frozen
salt and pepper to taste
1 onion, quartered
1 carrot, cut into chunks

1 tart apple, cored and quartered
Optional: chopped fresh parsley,
   sage and/or thyme
1/2 c. butter, melted and divided

Remove giblets and neck from inside turkey. Place turkey in a roasting
pan; pat dry with paper towels. Generously season turkey inside and
out with salt and pepper. Place remaining ingredients except butter
inside turkey. Brush melted butter over turkey. Tent with aluminum
foil. Bake at 325 degrees for 2 hours. Remove foil; brush with
remaining butter. Increase oven to 425 degrees. Bake, uncovered,
for one additional hour, or until a meat thermometer inserted in the
thigh reads 165 degrees. Transfer turkey to a platter; let stand about
15 minutes before carving. Serves 10 to 12.

Homemade pan gravy is delicious and easy to make. Remove the
roast turkey to a platter. Set the roasting pan with pan juices over
medium heat. Shake together 1/4 cup cold water and 1/4 cup
cornstarch in a small jar and pour into the pan. Cook and stir
until gravy comes to a boil and thickens, 5 to 10 minutes.
Season with salt and pepper, and it's ready to serve.

DOWN-HOME
Dinners to Share

Amanda's Turkey Casserole

Beth Smith
Manchester, MI

This recipe brings back so many wonderful memories! My grandmother made this every year on the day after Thanksgiving. I looked forward to it as much as the traditional Thanksgiving dinner. Thirty years ago, she gave me the recipe as part of my wedding shower gift. Now as I make it for my family, I think of my grandmother every time.

8-oz. pkg. elbow macaroni,
    uncooked
2 c. cooked turkey, cubed
1/2 c. onion, chopped
2 10-3/4 oz. cans cream of
    mushroom soup

2 c. milk
4 eggs, hard-boiled, peeled
    and sliced
3 T. butter, melted
1/2 c. buttery round crackers,
    crushed

In a large bowl, combine uncooked macaroni, turkey, onion, soup and milk. Mix well; transfer to a greased 3-quart casserole dish. Arrange sliced eggs over top. Mix crushed crackers with melted butter; sprinkle cracker mixture on top. Bake, uncovered, at 350 degrees for 1-1/2 hours, or until hot and bubbly. Serves 6 to 8.

Dress up stemmed glasses in a jiffy. Cut or tear fabric into 1/2-inch wide strips and tie a length around the stem of the glass. Choose team colors for game-day parties, harvest shades for Thanksgiving...the sky's the limit!

Game Board Night Casserole

Sandy Coffey
Cincinnati, OH

*Whenever we have family over to play board games, this recipe
is super easy and super good. Serve with warm rolls and
celery sticks. Now let the games begin!*

10-3/4 oz. can cream of chicken
    or celery soup
1/2 c. mayonnaise
1/2 c. milk
garlic powder, salt and pepper
    to taste
2 c. cooked chicken, cubed
1/2 c. carrot, peeled and grated

20-oz. pkg. frozen diced
    hashbrown potatoes
1 c. canned cut green beans,
    drained
3/4 c. shredded Cheddar cheese
1/2 c. seasoned dry bread
    crumbs

In a large bowl, stir together soup, mayonnaise, milk and seasonings.
Stir in chicken, carrot, potatoes and beans. Transfer to a lightly greased
13"x9" baking pan. Sprinkle cheese and bread crumbs on top. Bake,
uncovered, at 400 degrees for 40 minutes, or until hot and bubbly.
Serves 8.

Our annual trip with the kids to a local apple orchard was always
a fun family day. We ate apples from every row until our bags and
tummies were full. The sibling rivalry of picking the biggest apple
of the day was fun to watch. As the kids got older and could drag
the bags themselves through the rows of apples, it made my job
easier. Well, until we got home and I had to begin the wonderful
chore of making homemade applesauce! Now the children are
grown, and I take our grandsons to an orchard. It is wonderful
seeing our children's children making the same memories. Apple
picking will always be my favorite activity...it makes me feel
like a kid again.

–Kim Lamb, Taylorsville, KY

Chicken Taco Casserole

Tamatha Knauber
Lancaster, NY

This dish always makes me think of eating chicken tacos, hence the name. It is so yummy! Garnish with chopped tomato, green onion and cilantro before serving, if desired.

2 10-3/4 oz. cans cream of
   chicken soup
8-oz. container sour cream
4 c. cooked chicken, shredded
10-oz. can diced tomatoes with
   green chiles
15-1/2 oz. can black beans,
   drained and rinsed

1-oz. pkg. reduced-sodium taco
   seasoning mix
5 c. tortilla chips, coarsely
   crushed and divided
8-oz. pkg. shredded Cheddar
   cheese, divided

In a large bowl, stir together soup, sour cream, chicken, tomatoes with juice, beans and taco seasoning. Spread half of soup mixture in a lightly greased 13"x9" baking pan. Layer with 3 cups tortilla chips and one cup cheese. Layer with remaining soup mixture and tortilla chips. Cover and bake at 350 degrees for 30 minutes. Uncover and sprinkle with remaining cheese. Bake, uncovered, for 10 minutes, or until hot, bubbly and cheese is melted. Serves 8.

Hosting a crowd for a tailgating supper? Serve festive Mexican or Italian-style dishes that everybody loves. They usually feature rice or pasta, so they're filling yet budget-friendly. You can't go wrong!

Fusilli with Tomatoes & Zucchini

Lynne Almasy
Hubbard, OH

We raise our own meat and vegetables. I love making this dish for guests because we raise all the ingredients except the pasta. The sausage and veggies may be baked ahead of time, combined in a large pot and covered. Shortly before dinnertime, cook the pasta and top with warmed sausage mixture.

1 lb. sweet Italian pork
    sausage link
5 ripe tomatoes, diced
2 zucchini, halved lengthwise
    and sliced 1/4-inch thick
3/4 c. onion diced
3 cloves garlic, chopped
1/4 c. olive oil

1 t. salt
1/8 t. pepper
1/4 c. fresh basil, snipped
16-oz. pkg. fusilli pasta,
    uncooked
Garnish: shredded Parmesan
    cheese

Place sausage on an ungreased rimmed baking sheet. Bake at 350 degrees for 25 minutes. Cool; cut into one-inch pieces and set aside. Place vegetables on a rimmed baking sheet coated with non-stick vegetable spray. Drizzle with olive oil; sprinkle with salt, pepper and basil. Bake at 425 degrees for 20 minutes, or until vegetables are soft. Cook pasta according to package directions; drain. To serve, top pasta with sausage and vegetables. Serve with cheese on the side. Makes 6 servings.

Lay a blank card on each dinner plate and invite guests
of all ages to write down what they are most thankful for
this year. Afterwards, bind the cards together with a
ribbon to create a sweet gratitude book.

Mother's Baked Ziti

Maria Kuhns
Crofton, MD

My mother made this dish often when I was a child, using the overabundance of tomatoes and peppers grown in my father's vegetable garden. It's robust yet simple. Just add a garden salad and some warm bread for a complete meal.

2 T. extra virgin olive oil
1/2 c. onion, finely chopped
1 clove garlic, minced
1 green pepper, finely chopped
1 lb. lean ground beef
2 15-oz. cans tomato sauce
1 t. sugar

1 t. dried basil
1 t. dried oregano
1/2 t. salt
1/2 t. pepper
2 c. ziti pasta, uncooked
8-oz. pkg. shredded mozzarella
   cheese

Heat olive oil in a large skillet over medium heat for one minute. Add onion and garlic; cook for 5 minutes, until onion is translucent. Add green pepper and cook until softened, about 5 minutes. Add beef and cook until no longer pink; drain. Add tomato sauce, sugar and seasonings. Simmer over low heat until mixture is heated through; stirring occasionally, about 20 minutes. Meanwhile, cook pasta according to package directions. Drain pasta and stir into sauce. Add cheese; let stand for 5 minutes and serve. Makes 6 servings.

Let the children help out with the Thanksgiving feast. Something as simple as folding the napkins and setting the table means time spent together making memories.

Corn & Broccoli Calzones

Tonya Sheppard
Galveston, TX

I have a great recipe for sausage calzones that I make whenever my teenage son has his friends come over to play board games. For his vegetarian friends, I tried this veggie-packed version...it was a hit!

1-1/2 c. frozen corn, thawed
1-1/2 c. broccoli, chopped
1 c. shredded mozzarella cheese
2/3 c. ricotta cheese
4 green onions, thinly sliced
1/4 c. fresh basil, chopped

1/2 t. garlic powder
1/4 t. salt
1/4 t. pepper
20-oz. pkg. pizza dough,
   thawed if frozen
2 t. canola oil

In a large bowl, combine all ingredients except dough and oil; set aside. Divide dough into 6 pieces. On a floured surface, roll out each piece into an 8-inch circle. For each calzone, spoon 3/4 cup filling onto half of a dough circle, leaving a one-inch edge uncovered. Brush the edge with water; fold top half over the filling. Fold edges over; seal with a fork. Make several small slits in the top to vent; brush with oil. Divide calzones between 2 greased baking sheets. Position oven racks in upper and lower thirds of oven. Bake at 475 degrees for 15 minutes, or until golden, switching baking sheets between racks after 8 minutes. Let cool slightly before serving. Makes 6 servings.

Make-your-own sandwiches are perfect fare for casual get-togethers. Along with a platter of deli meats and cheeses, offer a variety of breads, rolls and buns. Keep them soft and fresh by arranging in a market basket, then covering with tea towels in harvest covers.

DOWN-HOME
Dinners to Share

Slow-Cooker Zesty Italian Beef

Beth Flack
Terre Haute, IN

A family favorite for football season. So simple to make!

4 to 5-lb. boneless beef
    rump roast
2 t. garlic powder
2 t. Italian seasoning
1 T. white vinegar
2 cubes beef bouillon

1 c. boiling water
1/2 c. onion, chopped
12-oz. jar pepperoncini peppers
French bread rolls, split
Garnish: provolone cheese slices

Put roast in a 6-quart slow cooker. Sprinkle with seasonings; drizzle with vinegar. Dissolve bouillon cubes in boiling water; pour over roast. Add onion and peppers with liquid. Cover and cook on low setting for 9 to 10 hours, until beef is very tender. Shred beef with 2 forks. Serve shredded beef on rolls, topped with provolone cheese. Serves 6.

Pack a tailgating kit for the trunk. Fill a tote bag with paper towels, wet wipes, trash bags, a bottle opener and matches for the grill... all those must-haves that are so easy to forget. Now enjoy your game day knowing that you're ready for anything!

Turkey & Pierogie Casserole

Carolyn Tellers
Erie, PA

This was inspired by an old family favorite...potato tot casserole.
I wanted to change it up with pierogies and lots of veggies.

1 lb. ground turkey
1/2 c. onion, chopped
1 to 2 zucchini, diced
3 stalks celery, chopped
15-1/2 oz. can black beans
15-1/2 oz. can cannellini beans
2 10-3/4 oz. cans cream of
   mushroom soup

1 c. shredded Cheddar cheese
4 slices turkey bacon, chopped
13-oz. pkg. frozen mini or
   regular white Cheddar
   pierogies, uncooked

Spread uncooked turkey in a lightly greased 13"x9" glass baking pan.
Layer with onion, zucchini, celery and beans. Spread with both cans
of soup. Sprinkle with cheese and uncooked bacon. Arrange pierogies
on top. Bake, uncovered, at 350 degrees for 40 minutes, or until
pierogies are golden. Flip pierogies over. Bake for an additional
20 minutes, or until hot and bubbly. Makes 6 to 8 servings.

Serve up an easy punch at the harvest table. Scoop 8 balls of
lemon or raspberry sherbet and freeze until serving time.
To serve, place each ball in a frosted stemmed glass. Carefully
pour 1/2 cup chilled cranberry juice cocktail over the
sherbet and garnish with a sprig of fresh mint.

Apple-Mustard Sauce Pork Chops

Donna Wilson
Maryville, TN

I created this for my family after looking over some recipe ideas. I wanted a quick autumn-flavored sauce and this is the result. It smells amazing as it cooks!

6 thinly sliced pork chops
salt and pepper to taste
1/4 c. butter
1 c. apple juice
1/2 c. applesauce
3 T. Dijon mustard

2 T. all-purpose flour
2 T. dried minced onion
1 t. onion powder
1/8 t. cinnamon
cooked rice

Season pork chops on both sides with salt and pepper. Melt butter in a large skillet over medium heat. Add chops; cook until golden on both sides. Remove from skillet; set aside on a plate. Add apple juice to skillet; gradually add remaining ingredients except rice. Cook and stir over medium heat until mixture thickens slightly. Return pork chops to skillet; reduce heat to low. Cover and cook for 10 minutes. Serve pork chops and sauce over cooked rice. Makes 6 servings.

Create a beautiful fall centerpiece in a snap! Hot-glue brightly colored ears of mini Indian corn around a terra-cotta pot and set a vase of orange or yellow mums in the center.

Apple-Glazed Pork Tenderloin
Nancy Levernier
Milford, IN

*This is one of the yummy recipes we've always prepared
at our girls' week at a cabin in Tennessee.*

1 lb. pork tenderloin
3/4 c. apple jelly
2 T. lemon juice

1/2 t. pumpkin pie spice
2 tart red apples, cored and
   thinly sliced

Place tenderloin in a roasting pan sprayed with non-stick vegetable spray; set aside. In a small bowl, combine apple jelly, lemon juice and spice; blend well. Brush tenderloin with half of jelly mixture. Bake, uncovered, at 375 degrees for 20 to 30 minutes, until a meat thermometer inserted in thickest part reads 160 degrees. Remove from oven; cover and let stand for several minutes. Line a broiler pan with aluminum foil; spray with non-stick vegetable spray. Arrange apple slices on broiler pan; brush with remaining jelly mixture. Broil for 5 to 6 minutes, until tender. Slice tenderloin and serve topped with apple slices. Makes 4 servings.

Decorate the house in unexpected places...a golden ribbon
around a stack of Shaker boxes, a garland of autumn leaves
around the hallway mirror and even a bow or two on
the backs of the dining room chairs.

Yummy Ham & Sweet Potatoes

Linda Smith
Fountain Hills, AZ

One of my family's favorite slow-cooker recipes for fall! It's very easy to make and tastes wonderful. Currently I'm cooking for just my husband and myself...this recipe is just right for the two of us.

2 to 4 small sweet potatoes
1-1/2 lb. boneless ham

1/4 c. brown sugar, packed
1/2 t. dry mustard

Place unpeeled sweet potatoes in a 4-quart slow cooker. Place ham on top. Blend together brown sugar and mustard; spread over ham. Cover and cook on low setting for 3 to 6 hours, until sweet potatoes are tender and a meat thermometer inserted in thickest part of ham reads 145 degrees. To serve, peel sweet potatoes, if desired. Slice ham and sweet potatoes; serve topped with juices from slow cooker. Makes 2 to 4 servings.

Show your spirit...dress up a garden scarecrow in
a hometown football jersey. Go team!

Mexican-Style Chicken & Rice

Sue Klapper
Muskego, WI

This recipe is a great combination of vegetables, chicken and rice. You don't even need to cook the rice! Serve with a dollop of sour cream.

3/4 c. onion, chopped
1 green pepper, chopped
1 to 2 t. oil
14-1/2 oz. can diced tomatoes
4-oz. can chopped green chiles
14-1/2 oz. can chicken broth
1-3/4 c. quick-cooking brown
    rice, uncooked

6 drops hot pepper sauce
1 t. garlic, minced
2 lbs. boneless, skinless chicken
    breasts
1/2 c. shredded Cheddar cheese

In a skillet over medium heat, cook onion and pepper in oil until tender. Add tomatoes with juice, chiles, broth, rice, hot sauce and garlic. Mix well and bring to a boil. Remove from heat; spoon into a lightly greased 13"x9" baking pan. Arrange chicken on top. Cover tightly with aluminum foil. Bake at 350 degrees for 35 minutes, or until rice is tender and chicken juices run clear. Sprinkle cheese on top. Let stand 5 minutes, or until cheese is melted. Makes 8 servings.

A fresh-tasting chopped salad of lettuce and tomatoes is always welcome alongside spicy Mexican dishes. Try this easy dressing. In a covered jar, combine 3 tablespoons olive oil, 2 tablespoons lime juice, 1/4 teaspoon dry mustard and 1/2 teaspoon salt. Cover and shake until well blended.

Dinners to Share

Mexican Vegetable Casserole

Kathy Scott
Corbin, KY

Super easy! Just add crusty bread or flour tortillas to make this meatless dish a complete meal.

15-1/2 oz. black beans, drained and rinsed
14-1/4 oz. can corn, drained
10-oz. can diced tomatoes with green chiles
8-oz. container sour cream
8-oz. jar chunky salsa
2 c. cooked brown rice

8-oz. pkg. shredded Cheddar cheese
1/4 t. pepper
4-oz. can sliced black olives, drained
8-oz. pkg. shredded Pepper Jack cheese

Combine all ingredients except olives and Pepper Jack cheese; mix well. Transfer to a lightly greased 13"x9" baking pan. Sprinkle with olives and Pepper Jack cheese. Bake, uncovered, at 350 degrees for 45 minutes, or until bubbly and cheese is melted. Makes 6 to 8 servings.

Decorative copper bowls and mugs pair nicely with table coverings and napkins in fall colors of gold, brown and orange.

One-Pan Chicken Dinner

Laura Fuller
Fort Wayne, IN

A delicious meal my family just loves! Sometimes I'll add some spears of fresh broccolini to the pan in the last step, after the oven temperature is raised. If you don't have a large jelly-roll pan, you can divide the ingredients between two 13"x9" baking sheets.

10 bone-in chicken thighs
    and drumsticks
2 T. olive oil
1 t. garlic powder
1 t. onion powder
1 t. salt

1 t. pepper
3 lbs. fingerling potatoes
1-1/2 c. buttermilk ranch salad
    dressing, divided
salt to taste

In a large bowl, drizzle chicken pieces with oil; sprinkle with seasonings and toss to coat well. Arrange chicken on an oiled 15"x10" jelly-roll pan. Bake at 325 degrees for 45 minutes. Arrange potatoes around chicken; bake for another 30 minutes. Spoon 3/4 cup salad dressing over all; season potatoes with salt. Return to oven for another 30 minutes. Spoon remaining dressing over all. Increase oven temperature to 375 degrees. Continue baking for 20 to 30 minutes, until chicken is golden and potatoes are tender. Serves 6 to 8.

Cut down on kitchen chores with a roll of heavy-duty aluminum foil. Line baking pans or sheets when fixing oven-baked chicken or pork chops, then toss away the mess. If your favorite casserole tends to drip or bubble over in the oven, place a sheet of foil under the pan to catch drippings. Clean-up's a snap!

DOWN-HOME
Dinners to Share

Cornish Hens with Peach Sauce

Deborah Patterson
Carmichael, CA

This is a lovely main dish for that special dinner for two.
When they're available, I use fresh ripe peaches and
mash about an extra cup of them for the syrup.

2 22-oz. frozen Cornish hens,
    thawed
salt and pepper to taste
16-oz. can sliced peaches in
    syrup, drained and 1/3 cup
    syrup reserved

2/3 c. orange juice
1 T. cornstarch
1/8 t. cinnamon

Place Cornish hens in a lightly greased 13"x9" baking pan. Season inside and out with salt and pepper; set aside. In a saucepan, combine peaches, reserved peach syrup and remaining ingredients. Simmer over medium heat for 5 minutes, or until slightly thickened. Set aside one cup peach sauce. Spoon remaining sauce over hens. Bake, uncovered, at 350 degrees for one hour to one hour and 15 minutes, until juices run clear and a meat thermometer inserted in thickest part reads 180 degrees. Increase oven to 400 degrees. Spoon reserved sauce over hens; bake another 10 minutes, until golden. Serves 2 to 4.

Mini tarts are just right after a hearty Thanksgiving dinner. With a 4-inch biscuit cutter, cut 6 circles from a pie crust. Press gently into ungreased muffin cups. Spoon 2 tablespoons apple or cherry pie filling into each cup. Bake at 425 degrees for 14 to 18 minutes, until bubbly and golden. So sweet!

Slow-Cooker Herbed Italian Beef

Wendy Ball
Battle Creek, MI

Always finding something different to do with beef roasts, I adapted this recipe for the slow cooker. Serve on good Italian rolls, garnished with shredded provolone cheese, grilled peppers & onions and maybe some horseradish mayonnaise. Outstanding!

3 to 4-lb. beef rump roast
2-1/2 c. water
8-oz. can can tomato sauce
1 t. Worcestershire sauce
1/2 t. low-sodium soy sauce
1-oz. pkg. Italian salad
    dressing mix
1 t. garlic powder

1 t. dried parsley
1 t. dried basil
1 t. dried oregano
1/2 t. salt
1 t. pepper
8 to 10 Italian rolls, split
    and toasted

Place roast in a 5-quart slow cooker; set aside. In a bowl, combine remaining ingredients except rolls; mix well and spoon over roast. Cover and cook on low setting for 6 to 8 hours. Remove roast to a platter; pull apart to shreds using 2 forks. Return roast to slow cooker; cook for another 1-1/2 to 2 hours. Serve shredded beef on toasted Italian rolls. Makes 8 to 10 servings.

Slow cookers are super year 'round...no matter what the occasion. So grab a friend and head out to a local craft show, barn sale or small-town county fair. When you come home, a delicious meal will be waiting for you!

Dinners to Share

Delicious Cola Roast

Michelle Powell
Valley, AL

Easiest roast ever...and it turns out perfect every time! Makes great barbecue-like sandwiches. Great to make ahead because it tastes even better the second day. A tailgating favorite!

4-lb. beef chuck or rump roast
garlic powder, salt and pepper
   to taste
3 T. oil
1-1/2 c. cola

12-oz. bottle chili sauce
1/4 c. Worcestershire sauce
3 T. hot pepper sauce, or to taste
16 sandwich buns, split

With a sharp knife, score roast in several places. Fill each slit with salt, pepper and garlic powder. Heat oil in a Dutch oven over medium-high heat. Add roast and brown on all sides. Pour cola and sauces over roast. Cover and bake at 325 degrees for 3 hours, or until very tender. Spoon onto buns. Makes 16 servings.

Slow-Cooker French Dip Sandwiches

Angie Darby
Gresham, OR

My family loves this slow-cooked roast after a night of football and cheer practices. After cooking all day, it takes me only minutes for me to put the finishing touches together.

2 to 3-lb. beef chuck or bottom
   round roast
2 10-1/2 oz. cans beef broth
1.35-oz. pkg. onion soup mix

6 hoagie rolls, split
softened butter to taste
6 slices provolone cheese

Place roast in a 4-quart slow cooker. Pour beef broth into a bowl; stir in soup mix. Pour mixture over roast. Cover and cook on low setting for 6 to 8 hours, or on high setting for 4 to 6 hours. Remove roast to a cutting board. Let stand for 20 minutes; slice. Spread hoagie rolls with butter. Top rolls with slices of beef and cheese. On a broiler pan, broil sandwiches until cheese is bubbly and edges of bread start to turn golden. Serve with sauce from slow cooker for dipping. Makes 6 to 8 servings.

Meatless Taco Bowls

Beverley Williams
San Antonio, TX

This slow-cooker recipe comes together in almost no time at all! We love to eat these tasty bowls for meatless Mondays. Add other favorite toppings you like...for example, diced tomato, chopped green onion and sliced black olives.

2 c. water
2 10-oz. cans diced tomatoes
   with green chiles
15-oz. can tomato sauce
15-1/4 oz. corn, drained
15-1/2 oz. can black beans,
   drained and rinsed

1-1/4 oz. pkg. taco seasoning
   mix
1-1/2 c. instant rice, uncooked
6 corn tortilla bowls
1-1/2 c. shredded Mexican-
   blend cheese
Optional: 6 T. sour cream

In a 4-quart slow cooker, combine water, tomatoes with juice, tomato sauce, corn, beans, taco seasoning and uncooked rice. Stir to mix well. Cover and cook on high setting for 2 hours, stirring occasionally. Serve mixture in tortilla bowls, topped with cheese and sour cream as desired. Makes 6 servings.

Maureen's Miracle Fish

Angela Acker
Nova Scotia, Canada

My Aunt Maureen gave me this tasty recipe years ago.
Use cheese-flavored crackers for extra flavor.

4 4-oz. haddock fillets
1/2 c. mayonnaise-type salad
   dressing

1 sleeve round buttery crackers,
   finely crushed
3 T. butter, diced

Pat fillets dry. Coat fillets with salad dressing; roll in crushed crackers. Arrange on a greased or parchment paper-lined baking sheet. Dot with butter. Bake at 350 degrees for 20 minutes, or until fish flakes easily with a fork. Makes 4 servings.

Dress up table settings in a snap...
tuck a sprig of fragrant herbs
into each napkin ring.

Shrimp & Zucchini Boats

Scarlett Hedden
Titusville, FL

My granny taught me this recipe. It's a great-tasting main dish, or you could make them smaller and serve as a side dish.

8 small zucchini, halved
    lengthwise
1 T. olive oil
1 onion, chopped
1 clove garlic, chopped
4 tomatoes, chopped
2 drops hot pepper sauce

1 t. dried thyme
salt and pepper to taste
10 large cooked shrimp, peeled
    and chopped
2 T. finely shredded mozzarella
    or Parmesan cheese

From each zucchini half, scoop out the pulp, creating a shell. Chop pulp and set aside. Heat oil in a skillet over medium heat. Cook onion until tender; add garlic and cook one more minute. Add zucchini pulp, tomatoes, hot sauce and seasonings. Simmer for 10 minutes. Stir in shrimp. Spoon mixture into shells. Arrange on a lightly greased baking sheet; cover with aluminum foil. Bake at 400 degrees for 15 minutes. Uncover; sprinkle cheese over shells. Bake for another 5 minutes, or until cheese melts. Serve 8.

Younger guests will feel so grown up when served bubbly sparkling cider or ginger ale in long-stemmed plastic glasses. Decorate with ribbon just for fun.

Kathy's Chicken Creation

Kathy Greever
Mountain City, TN

I just tossed together some ingredients and came up with this...
it is delicious! This freezes well, or leftovers make
a great lunch the next day.

16-oz. pkg. rotini pasta or elbow
   macaroni, uncooked
16-oz. container cottage cheese
2 c. grated Parmesan cheese
2 t. water
8-oz. jar mild salsa
16-oz. pkg. grilled and carved
   chicken breast, cut into
   bite-size pieces

2 c. Alfredo sauce
8-oz. pkg. shredded Cheddar
   cheese
1/8 t. salt
1/8 t. pepper

Cook pasta according to package directions; drain. Meanwhile, combine cottage cheese, Parmesan cheese and water in a bowl; stir well and set aside. In a greased 13"x9" baking pan: layer 1/3 each of cooked pasta, cottage cheese mixture, salsa, chicken, Alfredo sauce and Cheddar cheese. Repeat layering twice, adding salt and pepper before adding Cheddar cheese. Bake, uncovered, at 350 degrees for 20 to 25 minutes, until hot and bubbly. Serves 8.

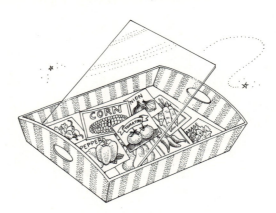

Look for old seed packets at flea markets...they're inexpensive and such fun to spread out on a serving tray! Cover them with a protective piece of glass cut to fit.

DOWN-HOME
Dinners to Share

Chicken Tetrazzini

Ann Davis
Brookville, IN

My kids love this...they always devour their helpings!

16-oz. pkg. linguine pasta,
  uncooked
5 boneless, skinless chicken
  breasts, cooked and
  shredded
2 10-3/4 oz. cans cream of
  chicken soup
16-oz. container sour cream

1/3 c. butter, melted
1/2 c. chicken broth
1/2 t. salt
1/2 t. pepper
2 T. grated Parmesan cheese
8-oz. pkg. shredded mozzarella
  cheese
2 T. fresh parsley, chopped

Cook pasta according to package instructions; drain. Meanwhile, in a
large bowl, combine remaining ingredients except cheeses and parsley.
Stir in cooked pasta. Transfer mixture to a 13"x9" baking pan sprayed
with non-stick vegetable spray. Sprinkle with cheeses; top with parsley.
Cover with aluminum foil. Bake at 300 degrees for 45 minutes.
Remove foil; bake for an additional 10 to 15 minutes, until bubbly
and cheese is melted. Serves 8.

The crackle of a warm, cozy fire brings everyone together.
Enjoy a simple dinner of roasted hot dogs or toasty pie-iron
sandwiches, then make s'mores and serve mugs of warm
spiced cider. Memories in the making!

Apple-Raisin Pork Tenderloin

Billie Jean Elliott
Woodsfield, OH

My son and his wife were building a new home, so to help them out, I did some cooking for them. I baked this tenderloin and it was the best ever...it certainly was most welcome at their dinner table. Quite a twist for the ordinary roasted tenderloin!

2 to 3-lb. pork tenderloin	2 T. all-purpose flour
1/2 t. ground sage	1/2 c. brown sugar, packed
1/2 t. salt	1 c. orange juice
1/2 t. pepper	1 T. vinegar
3 McIntosh apples, peeled, cored and diced	1/2 to 3/4 c. raisins

Place tenderloin in a lightly greased roasting pan. Combine seasonings; rub over tenderloin. Bake, uncovered, at 350 degrees for 30 to 40 minutes. Combine remaining ingredients; spoon over roast. Bake an additional 30 minutes, basting several times with pan juices, until a meat thermometer inserted in the thickest part reads 170 degrees. Makes 6 servings.

While you're adding the finishing touches to a big holiday meal, set out a nutcracker with a bowl of nuts in the shell for guests to enjoy. Before they know it, dinner is served!

Pork Chops with Cranberry-Orange Sauce

Mary Thomason-Smith
Bloomington, IN

*Perfect when you're going to spend an autumn day on a leaf walk...
or on raking leaves! Serve with ready-made stuffing mix and steamed
broccoli for an easy and appealing autumn meal that hints of
Thanksgiving dinner.*

4 boneless pork chops
1/2 c. sweet onion, chopped
1/4 c. fresh thyme, chopped
15-oz. can whole-berry
   cranberry sauce

1/2 c. apple juice
3 T. butter, melted
zest of 1 orange
juice of 1/2 orange

Arrange pork chops in a 3-quart slow cooker. Cover with onion and
thyme; set aside. In a small bowl, mix together remaining ingredients;
spoon over pork chops. Cover and cook on low setting for 5 to
6 hours, until pork chops are tender. Makes 4 servings.

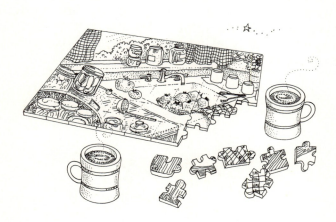

Family night! Serve a simple supper, then spend the
evening assembling jigsaw puzzles or playing favorite
board games together.

Savory Pot Roast Dinner

Julie Harris
Mertztown, PA

This is my go-to recipe for Sunday dinner. It's so quick & easy to toss all the ingredients into the slow cooker in the morning before heading out to church. You'll have a perfect meal ready for you when you walk back through your door. Not to mention the scrumptious smell that will greet you upon arrival!

1 T. butter, melted
1 c. onion, coarsely chopped
    and divided
6 carrots, peeled, coarsely
    chopped and divided
4 stalks celery, coarsely chopped
    and divided
2 1-oz. pkgs. brown gravy mix,
    divided

5-lb. beef chuck roast
1 c. warm water
1.35-oz. pkg. onion soup mix
salt and pepper to taste
5 to 6 potatoes, peeled and
    chopped

Spread melted butter in a 6-quart slow cooker. Add half each of onion, carrots and celery. Sprinkle one packet of gravy mix over vegetables; place roast on top. Drizzle warm water over roast. Sprinkle roast with soup mix, remaining gravy mix, salt and pepper. Arrange potatoes and remaining vegetables around roast. Cover and cook on high setting for 4 to 6 hours, until roast is falling-apart tender and vegetables are fork-tender. Serves 6 to 8.

Invite friends to join you for a favorite slow-cooker or skillet meal...a meal shared with friends doesn't need to be fancy. After all, it's friendship that makes it special!

Favorite Roast Beef

Elizabeth Smithson
Cunningham, KY

*A dear friend gave me this slow-cooker recipe years ago, and it
became a favorite of my family. It's excellent for sandwiches,
or add a salad and some Mexican corn for dinner.*

4 to 5-lb. beef chuck roast
salt and pepper to taste
4 cubes beef bouillon
4 jarred jalapeño or pepperoncini
  peppers, chopped

12-oz. can regular or
  non-alcoholic beer
1 T. Italian seasoning
1 t. garlic powder

Season roast on all sides with salt and pepper; place in a 6-quart slow
cooker. Tuck bouillon cubes around roast; place peppers on top. Drizzle
beer over roast; sprinkle with seasonings. Cover and cook on low
setting for 6 to 8 hours, until roast is tender. Makes 6 to 8 servings.

Some well-loved friends who are my family, Paula and her husband
Tim, used to make some wonderful memories for all of their family
& friends. They always had a big fall party, full of food and games
for all. They made sure to have games and prizes for all the kids of
all ages...even adults! Paula is so talented that she'd have craft
stations going for all the different age groups. She and Tim would
have 3 or 4 soups simmering, with so much more food than could
be eaten. Paula loves to decorate for fall, so every room in the
house was in full fall colors. She always had scented candles
burning so it smelled wonderful. While their three boys keep them
too busy for parties now, I will always have my favorite memories
of those parties. They made everyone feel special.

–Karen Rearick, Apollo, PA

Spicy Shrimp Pasta

Michelle Powell
Valley, AL

Growing up on the Gulf Coast, we've eaten shrimp cooked a bazillion ways. This is one of our favorites! It's quick & easy, too.

8-oz. linguine pasta, uncooked
2 T. olive oil
1 jalapeño pepper, seeds
   removed, finely chopped
2 cloves garlic, minced
1/2 t. salt

1/4 t. pepper
1 lb. medium shrimp, thawed if
   frozen, peeled and deveined
2 c. ripe tomatoes, chopped
Garnish: grated Parmesan
   cheese

Cook pasta according to package directions; drain. Meanwhile, in a large skillet, heat oil over medium high heat. Add jalapeño, garlic, salt and pepper. Cook and stir for one minute. Add shrimp; cook about 3 minutes, until shrimp turn opaque. Stir in tomatoes; heat through. Add cooked pasta; toss with shrimp mixture. Top with a sprinkle of Parmesan cheese. Makes 4 servings.

Perfect Oven-Baked Tilapia

Victoria Mitchel
Gettysburg, PA

We all love fried fish, so I've experimented many times with different recipes. This recipe turns out crunchy and flaky... my family loves it! I serve it with fries and coleslaw.

1-1/2 c. cornmeal
1-1/2 c. panko crumbs
2-1/2 t. seasoning salt
1-1/2 t. garlic powder
1 t. Cajun seasoning

3 eggs, beaten
8 4 to 5-oz. tilapia fillets
2 to 4 T. butter, melted
Garnish: lemon slices, tartar
   sauce

In a bowl, combine panko crumbs, cornmeal and seasonings; set aside. Beat eggs in another bowl. Coat fish fillets in crumb mixture, coating both sides well. Dip into egg, letting any excess drip off; coat again in crumb mixture. Place fillets on a parchment paper-lined baking sheet. Drizzle with melted butter. Bake at 425 degrees for 15 to 20 minutes, until flaky. Serve warm, garnished as desired. Makes 6 to 8 servings.

DOWN-HOME
Dinners to Share

3-Cheese Zucchini Lasagna

Angela Bissette
Middlesex, NC

This recipe is a delicious, healthier version of my favorite comfort food. Served with a crisp tossed salad, it makes a complete, nutritious meal.

2 to 3 zucchini, ends trimmed
16-oz. container low-fat
    cottage cheese
8-oz. pkg. shredded mozzarella
    cheese
1 egg, beaten

2 24-oz. jars pasta sauce,
    divided
9 oven-ready lasagna noodles,
    uncooked
Optional: additional shredded
    mozzarella cheese

Cut zucchini lengthwise into 1/2-inch slices; add to a saucepan of boiling water. Cook for 5 minutes; drain and set side on paper towels. In a bowl, mix together cheeses and egg. Spread 1-1/2 cups of sauce in the bottom of a greased 13"x9" baking pan. Layer with 3 noodles, 1/3 of zucchini strips and 1/3 of cottage cheese mixture. Repeat layers, ending with sauce. Sprinkle with additional mozzarella cheese, if desired. Cover with aluminum foil. Bake at 350 degrees for one hour. Let stand 10 minutes before serving. Makes 8 servings.

Over dinner, ask your kids to tell you about books they're reading at school and return the favor by sharing books you loved as a child....perhaps stories of small-town life like *Anne of Green Gables* or *Little House on the Prairie*. You may find you have some favorites in common!

Skillet Turkey Chilaquiles

Angela Murphy
Tempe, AZ

It's good to know something different to do with leftover turkey! You may even have broken-up tortilla chips left after watching the big game on TV. Enjoy!

2 T. olive oil
1-1/2 c. red onion, diced
   and divided
2 c. cooked turkey, diced
4-oz. can diced green chiles
3 c. medium-hot salsa

salt and pepper to taste
4 c. tortilla chips, coarsely
   broken
2 c. shredded Mexican-blend
   cheese
Garnish: sour cream

In a large cast-iron skillet, heat olive oil over medium heat. Add 1-1/4 cups onion; cook until softened, about 5 minutes. Add turkey and chiles; cook for 3 minutes. Stir in salsa; simmer over low heat until heated through. Season with salt and pepper. Gently fold in tortilla chips; top with cheese. Transfer skillet to oven. Bake, uncovered, at 450 degrees for about 5 minutes, just until cheese melts. At serving time, sprinkle with remaining onion; dollop with sour cream. Makes 4 to 6 servings.

Fill a basket with all the groceries for a holiday dinner. Have the kids make a sign saying "Happy Thanksgiving from our family to yours" and deliver the basket to a neighborhood charity. A sure way to remember what Thanksgiving is all about!

FUN TREATS FOR
FOR
Festive Parties

Chocolate Crinkle Cookies

Mel Chencharick
Julian, PA

I remember getting these cookies as a child in my elementary school cafeteria. I always loved them. I searched and never found just the right recipe, but I think this is it, just like I remember.

1 c. powdered sugar
1 c. sugar
4 eggs, beaten
1 c. baking cocoa

2 c. all-purpose flour
2 t. baking powder
2 t. vanilla extract
1/4 c. butter, softened

Place powdered sugar in a small bowl; set aside. In a large bowl, combine remaining ingredients. Beat well with an electric mixer on medium speed. Form dough into balls by tablespoonfuls; roll in powdered sugar. Place on a parchment paper-lined baking sheet, about 2 inches apart. Bake at 350 degrees for 10 to 15 minutes. Makes 3 dozen.

Autumn is the perfect time of year to share some tasty treats with teachers, librarians and school bus drivers... let them know how much they're appreciated!

FUN TREATS FOR
Festive Parties

Peanut Butter & Jelly Bars

Lori Simmons
Princeville, IL

If your kids like peanut butter & jelly sandwiches, they will surely love these cookie bars! Kids especially like grape jelly and strawberry jam, but you can use any flavor.

16-1/2 oz. tube refrigerated
   peanut butter cookie dough
1/2 c. peanut butter chips

16-oz. can buttercream frosting
1/4 c. creamy peanut butter
1/4 c. favorite jam or jelly

Let dough soften for 5 to 10 minutes at room temperature. Press dough into an ungreased 13"x9" baking pan; sprinkle with peanut butter chips. Bake at 375 degrees for 15 to 18 minutes, until lightly golden and edges are firm to the touch. Remove from oven. In a small bowl, beat together frosting and peanut butter until smooth. Spread over bars. Drop jam over frosting by teaspoonfuls. Cut through frosting with a table knife to swirl jam. Cut into bars. Makes 2 dozen.

Clean-up is a snap for bar cookies. Just line the baking pan with aluminum foil before adding the dough, leaving a foil "handle" extending on each side. Once the cookies have completely cooled, lift out the cookies by the handles, peel off the foil and cut into bars.

Pumpkin-Oat Scotchies

Stefanie Fierro Arms
Gilbert, AZ

I have been enjoying this recipe for years! It really gets a cozy fall day off to a good start here in Arizona.

2 c. old-fashioned oats,
   uncooked
1 c. all-purpose flour
3/4 c. brown sugar, packed
1/2 c. butterscotch chips
1 t. baking soda
1/2 t. salt

1/2 t. pumpkin pie spice
1/2 t. cinnamon
3/4 c. butter, softened
1/2 c. sugar
1 egg, beaten
1/2 c. canned pumpkin
1 t. vanilla extract

In a bowl, combine oats, flour, brown sugar, butterscotch chips, baking soda, salt and spices. Mix well and set aside. In a large bowl, blend butter and sugar together. Add egg, pumpkin and vanilla; stir well. Add oat mixture to butter mixture; mix well. Scoop dough into one-inch balls. Place on ungreased baking sheets, 2 inches apart. Bake at 350 degrees for 10 minutes. Cool on wire racks. Makes 3 dozen.

When the temperature is dropping, treat yourself to a cup of warm mulled cider. Heat a mug of cider to boiling, add an orange spice teabag and let stand several minutes. Mmm!

FUN TREATS FOR
Festive Parties

Best Fall Cut-Out Cookies

Jean McKinney
Ontario, OH

These puffy golden cookies are a favorite...they bring back sweet memories. They keep for two months if frozen unfrosted.

1 c. butter, room temperature	3 c. all-purpose flour
1 c. sugar	1 t. baking powder
1/2 t. salt	1/2 t. baking soda
3 eggs, beaten	Garnish: frosting, candy
1 t. vanilla extract	sprinkles

In a large bowl, blend together butter, sugar, salt, eggs and vanilla; set aside. In a separate bowl, mix together flour, baking powder and baking soda. Slowly add flour mixture to butter mixture; stir well. Cover and refrigerate 2 hours to overnight. Roll out dough on a floured surface to 1/4-inch thick. Cut out with cookie cutters. Brush off any excess flour with a pastry brush; place cookies on parchment paper-covered baking sheets. Bake at 400 degrees for 5 minutes, or until very lightly golden and puffed up. Cookies bake fast, so watch closely. Cool; frost as desired. Makes about 2 dozen.

I grew up in a small town in Ohio in the 70s. Every fall, my class would be treated to a large pumpkin-shaped cut-out cookie from the town bakery and a small carton of orange juice. During my early childhood, the teachers gave us this treat in class. In 4th grade through 6th, we actually got to hike downtown as a class field trip and enjoy this treat at the bakery. This is my favorite fall memory always. Later in life, I took a class and found that several of my adult classmates shared that same memory. So one day another classmate and I surprised our adult class with pumpkin cut-out cookies from the bakery and orange juice. That day, we shared childhood memories of school days gone by. The bakery has been gone for some time now, but I'm happy I have a recipe that's close to those wonderful bakery cookies!

–Jean McKinney, Ontario, OH

Appledoodles

Katie Wollgast
Troy, MO

Snickerdoodles have been one of my favorites since my kindergarten teacher used to make them for us. This is a wonderful twist. They are so good in fall, served warm with a cold glass of milk. Rolling the little balls is fun for children and children at heart!

2-2/3 c. all-purpose flour
2 t. baking powder
1 t. cream of tartar
1/2 t. salt
1/2 t. cinnamon
1/2 t. nutmeg
1/2 c. butter, softened
3/4 c. sugar, divided

1/2 c. brown sugar, packed
2 eggs, beaten
1 t. vanilla extract
1 c. tart apple, peeled and
   shredded
1/2 c. walnuts, finely chopped
2 t. apple pie spice or additional
   cinnamon

In a bowl, combine flour, baking powder, cream of tartar, salt and spices; set aside. In a large bowl, blend butter, 1/2 cup sugar and brown sugar. Beat in eggs and vanilla. Add flour mixture to butter mixture; stir until moistened. Stir in apple and nuts. Combine remaining sugar and spice in a small bowl; set aside. With floured hands, roll dough into 48 smooth balls, about one inch. Coat balls with sugar mixture. Place balls on parchment paper-lined baking sheets, 2 inches apart. Bake at 350 degrees for 12 to 15 minutes, until lightly golden on the edges and barely set in the centers. Cool for 2 minutes; remove to wire racks to cool completely. Makes 4 dozen.

For delicious apple pies and cakes, some of the best apple varieties are Granny Smith, Gala and Jonathan as well as old-timers like Rome Beauty, Northern Spy & Winesap. Ask at the orchard...the grower is sure to have tips for you!

FUN TREATS FOR
Festive Parties

Trail Bars

Leona Krivda
Belle Vernon, PA

It's always nice to have a snack on a long day. These will hit the spot if you are driving on a trip to see the autumn colors, or hiking in the hills. I even like to have some on handy if I am just doing yardwork!

1 c. butter, softened	1 t. baking soda
1/2 c. sugar	1-1/2 c. rolled oats, uncooked
1/2 c. brown sugar, packed	6-oz. pkg. mini semi-sweet
2 eggs, beaten	chocolate chips
1 t. vanilla extract	1/2 c. sunflower seeds
1-1/4 c. all-purpose flour	1 c. pecan pieces

In a large bowl, blend butter and sugars very well. Blend in eggs and vanilla; set side. In a separate bowl, mix flour and baking soda; add to butter mixture. Stir in remaining ingredients. Press dough into a well-greased 13"x9" baking pan. Bake at 375 degrees for 25 to 30 minutes. Cool in pan on a wire rack; cut into bars. Makes one to 1-1/2 dozen.

Plan a harvest scavenger hunt for the whole family. Send them out with a list of fall finds...a golden oak leaf, a russet-red maple leaf, a pumpkin, a scarecrow, a red apple and a hay bale, just to name a few. It's not only lots of fun, it's a great way to get outside and enjoy the fabulous fall weather!

Toffee Bars

Sharon Larson
Collinsville, IL

This is a quick & easy recipe that I got from my church Bible study. It has been in my recipe box for more than 30 years. These bar cookies are always a hit, and everyone asks for the recipe. I always take home an empty container.

1 c. all-purpose flour
1-3/4 c. brown sugar, packed
   and divided
1/2 c. cold butter, cubed
1 egg, beaten

1 t. vanilla extract
1 t. baking powder
1 c. flaked coconut
1/2 c. chopped pecans or walnuts

In a large bowl, combine flour and 3/4 cup brown sugar. Cut in butter with a fork until crumbly. Press dough into an ungreased 13"x9" baking pan. Bake at 350 degrees for 8 to 10 minutes, until golden; cool slightly. In a small bowl, beat egg, remaining brown sugar, vanilla and baking powder until blended. Stir in coconut and pecans; spread over baked crust. Bake for another 12 to 15 minutes, until golden. Cool in pan on a wire rack; cut into bars. Makes 2 dozen.

Indoor S'mores

Barb Bargdill
Gooseberry Patch

Perfect on a rainy day! I like to cut them into bite-size morsels.

1/3 c. light corn syrup
1 T. butter
1 c. milk chocolate chips
1/2 t. vanilla extract

4 c. bite-size sweetened graham
   cereal squares
1-1/2 c. mini marshmallows

Combine corn syrup and butter in a large saucepan over medium heat. Heat to boiling; remove from heat. Add chocolate chips and vanilla; stir until melted. Fold in cereal gradually until well coated with chocolate; fold in marshmallows. Turn mixture into a buttered 9"x9" baking pan; smooth with back of spoon. Let stand at room temperature at least one hour; cut into bars. Makes 2 dozen.

No-Bake Corn Chip-Peanut Butter Squares

LaShelle Brown
Mulvane, KS

This sweet & salty crunchy treat is perfect for dessert or even to take to a tailgate party! It sounds like a very odd combination, but trust me, it's good. Every time I take this to a gathering, I am asked by numerous people for the recipe...and it couldn't be simpler.

10-1/4 oz. pkg. corn chips
1 c. light corn syrup

1 c. sugar
1 c. creamy peanut butter

Line a rimmed baking sheet with aluminum foil; spray with non-stick vegetable spray. Spread corn chips on baking sheet; set aside. In a saucepan over medium heat, bring corn syrup and sugar to a boil. Cook, stirring often, until sugar dissolves. Boil for one minute. Remove from heat; stir in peanut butter until smooth. Pour mixture over corn chips. Cool, cut into squares. Makes 2 dozen.

Make cookie giving fun...tuck a variety of wrapped cookies inside a pumpkin-shaped plastic pail. Remember to include copies of the recipes. All treats, no tricks!

Farmhouse Molasses Cookies

Brenda Huey
Geneva, IN

This is an old-fashioned favorite we always made on the farm. Now I make them every fall at our bakery.

2-1/4 c. sugar, divided
1-1/2 c. oil
2 eggs, beaten
1/2 c. molasses
4 c. all-purpose flour

4 t. baking soda
1 t. salt
1 T. ground ginger
2 t. cinnamon

In a bowl, combine 2 cups sugar, oil, eggs and molasses; mix well. Add remaining ingredients; mix until combined. Roll dough into one-inch balls; roll in remaining sugar. Place on ungreased baking sheets. Bake at 350 degrees for 8 to 10 minutes; cool on wire racks. Makes 2 dozen.

Some of my fondest memories of visits to my grandparents' home were in the kitchen. With five brothers, I was the only granddaughter, so Grandma would spend extra quality time with me. She loved to bake and taught me many of her baking tips. The Thanksgiving visits were one of my favorites, as we would spend an entire day baking loaves of pumpkin bread using fresh pumpkins. Many of the loaves would be gifts to neighbors and church friends.

I remember we wrapped some loaves festively with a ribbon for Grandma to sell at the church bazaar to raise money for their youth activities. I was proud to be a part of these baking experiences with Grandma. The fond memories that she gave me will remain with me always. The love of baking that she taught me was happily passed on to my children while I told stories of our special times together. Now that I am a grandmother myself, I look forward to being able to pass along special memories to my own granddaughter.

–Deborah Davis, Shortsville, NY

FUN TREATS FOR
Festive Parties

No-Bake Monster Oatmeal Bites

Stephanie Turner
Meridian, ID

This is a great snack for kids and adults alike. It's made with oats, protein-packed peanut butter, honey for sweetening and a little bit of chocolate. Keep some in the fridge for a quick bite any time you need it.

2-1/2 c. old-fashioned oats, uncooked
1 c. creamy or crunchy peanut butter
1/2 c. honey
1 t. vanilla extract

1/2 c. mini semi-sweet chocolate chips
1/2 c. mini candy-coated chocolates
Optional: 1/2 c. sweetened or unsweetened flaked coconut

In a large bowl, stir together all ingredients until well combined. Roll mixture into 1-1/2 inch balls. Place balls on parchment paper-lined baking sheets. Refrigerate for at least 30 minutes, until set. Transfer to an airtight container; keep refrigerated for one to 2 weeks. Makes about 3 dozen.

Sweet invitations! Decorate paper gift bags with Halloween stickers and paint...write the party details on one side of bag. Later, bags can be used for collecting treats.

Disappearing Popcorn Balls

Tracie Carlson
Richardson, TX

These disappear before your eyes! I've been making them for 40 years, and they are so good. I always make two batches, orange and grape for Halloween and cherry and lime for Christmas. All flavors are equally delicious. Sugar-free gelatin works fine too.

12 c. popped popcorn   1/2 c. sugar
1 c. light corn syrup   3-oz. pkg. favorite gelatin mix

Place popcorn in a large heatproof bowl; remove any unpopped kernels and set aside. Combine corn syrup and sugar in a heavy saucepan. Bring to a boil over medium-high heat, stirring often. Remove from heat. Add gelatin mix; stir until dissolved. Pour mixture over popcorn in bowl; stir gently until well mixed. When cool enough to handle, lightly butter your hands to prevent sticking; shape into 12 balls. Place each ball on a large square of wax paper and roll up; tie ends with ribbon to suit the occasion. Makes one dozen.

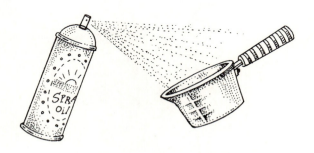

When measuring a sticky ingredient like corn syrup,
honey or peanut butter, spray the measuring cup with
non-stick vegetable spray first. It will all come out easily!

FUN TREATS FOR
Festive Parties

Toffee Brickle Popcorn

Katie Majeske
Denver, PA

We love popcorn and enjoy trying new combinations.
This is one of our favorites.

10 to 12 c. popped popcorn
1/2 c. sliced almonds
8-oz. pkg. toffee brickle
   baking bits
1 c. brown sugar, packed

1/2 c. butter
1/2 c. light corn syrup
1 t. almond extract
1/2 t. baking soda

Place popcorn in a greased large roasting pan; remove any unpopped kernels. Add almonds and brickle bits; toss to mix and set aside. In a saucepan, mix brown sugar, butter and corn syrup. Cook over medium heat, stirring until mixture boils. Boil without stirring for 5 minutes. Remove from heat. Add extract and baking soda; stir until foamy and light in color. Pour over popcorn mixture in pan; mix well. Bake at 250 degrees for 45 minutes, stirring every 15 minutes. Spread in a single layer on parchment paper to cool. Makes 8 to 10 servings.

For fun party favors, fill clear plastic cups with crunchy caramel popcorn. Seal with sheets of colorful plastic wrap to keep the goodies inside. Heap the cups in a basket...guests can choose a favorite to take home.

Pumpkin Seed Brittle

Lynda Robson
Boston, MA

After carving the Halloween Jack-o'-Lantern together, my kids and I wanted to do something different with the pumpkin seeds. This is quick, a little different and really tasty!

1 c. pumpkin seeds
1 T. oil
salt to taste
3/4 c. sugar
1/4 c. light corn syrup

1/4 c. water
1 T. butter
1/2 t. baking soda
1/2 t. vanilla extract

In a bowl, toss pumpkin seeds with oil and salt. Spread evenly in a shallow microwave-safe glass dish. Microwave on high for 5 minutes, stirring every minute. Microwave on medium for 8 minutes, stirring every 2 minutes, or until crisp. Set aside to cool; transfer to an 8-cup glass measuring cup. Add sugar, corn syrup and water. Microwave on high without stirring for 10 to 11 minutes, until medium-dark golden. Stir in butter, baking soda and vanilla. Immediately pour hot mixture onto a greased baking sheet; spread out evenly. Cool; break into chunks. Makes about 1-1/2 cups.

Thrift store lanterns and hurricane globes make wonderful Halloween party lighting...the shabbier, the better! Arrange in a large tabletop grouping and twine twinkling white or purple lights inside.

Pumpkin Spice Fudge

Carmen Hyde
Spencerville, IN

This recipe is scrumptious and perfect for fall. It's a much-requested favorite at our house!

3 c. sugar
3/4 c. butter
2/3 c. evaporated milk
1/2 c. canned pumpkin

1 t. pumpkin pie spice
12-oz. pkg. butterscotch chips
7-oz. jar marshmallow creme
1 t. vanilla extract

In a heavy large saucepan, combine sugar, butter, evaporated milk, pumpkin and spice. Bring to a boil over medium heat. Cook and stir until mixture reaches the soft-ball stage, or 230 to 235 degrees on a candy thermometer. Remove from heat; add butterscotch chips and stir until melted. Add marshmallow creme and vanilla; mix well. Pour into a buttered 13"x9" baking pan. Cool; cut into squares. Makes 2-1/2 dozen pieces.

Celebrate the spooky season...surround an orange pillar candle with candy corn in a glass hurricane.

Cranberry-White Chocolate Chunk Cookies

Jo Ann
Gooseberry Patch

Treat yourself and your family to these tender cookies. They're packed with fall-favorite cranberries and lots of chunks of white chocolate...yum!

2/3 c. butter, softened
2/3 c. brown sugar, packed
2 eggs
1-1/2 c. old-fashioned oats, uncooked
1-1/2 c. all-purpose flour

1 t. baking soda
1/2 t. salt
5-oz. pkg. sweetened dried cranberries
2/3 c. white chocolate chunks

Combine butter and brown sugar in a bowl. Beat with an electric mixer on medium speed until light and fluffy. Beat in eggs; set aside. In a separate bowl, combine oats, flour, baking soda and salt. Stir gradually into butter mixture. Stir in cranberries and chocolate chunks. Drop dough by rounded teaspoonfuls onto ungreased baking sheets. Bake at 375 degrees for 10 to 12 minutes, until golden. Cool on a wire rack. Makes 2-1/2 dozen.

Host a neighborhood spruce-up! Everyone can help rake leaves, trim bushes, pull bloomed-out annuals...kids can help too. Afterwards, share cider and doughnuts for a perfect ending to a fun get-together.

FUN TREATS FOR
Festive Parties

Apple Slice Bars

Sue Roberson-Haynes
Scottsdale, AZ

This recipe is so much fun to make! It's a favorite of mine that brings back memories of great times with great family & friends back in Wausau, Wisconsin.

2 14-oz. pkgs. refrigerated pie
   crusts, unbaked and divided
1 c. corn flake cereal, crushed
5 c. tart apples, peeled, cored
   and cut into bite-sized
   chunks

1-1/2 c. sugar
1 t. cinnamon, or more to taste
1 egg white
1 c. powdered sugar
2 T. lemon juice
1/8 t. white vinegar

Arrange 2 pie crusts side-by-side on an ungreased 15"x10" jelly-roll pan; press seam together. Spread crushed cereal over crusts; set aside. In a bowl, toss apples with sugar and cinnamon. Spread apple mixture evenly over cereal. Top with remaining 2 pie crusts; pinch edges together to seal. In a small bowl, beat egg white with an electric mixer on high until stiff peaks form; brush over crust. Bake at 350 degrees for 30 to 35 minutes. Cool slightly. Combine remaining ingredients; stir to a drizzling consistency and drizzle over crust. Cut into bars. Serve warm or cooled. Makes 2 dozen.

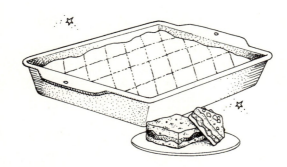

Need a dessert for a tailgating crowd? Bake up a jelly-roll pan recipe like Apple Slice Bars or chocolate sheet cake. These recipes make plenty of servings and are a snap to serve and clean up...sure to please everyone too!

Fall Family
• R E C I P E S •

Fall Snack Mix

Beth Adelson
Hastings, NE

A great recipe to take along for tailgates or fall get-togethers.

12-oz. pkg. bite-size crispy corn
   & rice cereal squares
2 c. English walnut halves
   or pieces
1 c. butter, melted

3/4 c. sugar
1 t. cinnamon
2 c. Granny Smith or other dried
   apples, coarsely chopped

Combine cereal and walnuts in a large heatproof bowl; set aside. In a separate bowl, combine butter, sugar and cinnamon. Pour over cereal mixture; stir to coat. Spread evenly on an ungreased 15"x11" jelly-roll pan. Bake at 250 degrees for 45 minutes, stirring every 15 minutes. Remove from oven; mix in apples when cool. Store in a covered container. Makes about 10 cups.

Haystacks

Becca Jones
Jackson, TN

This recipe is a favorite and so easy to make. A co-worker and friend used to make this treat for the office girls...they look like little haystacks! She was kind enough to share the recipe with us.

12-oz. pkg. butterscotch chips
5-oz. can chow mein noodles

8-oz. can salted cocktail peanuts

In a large saucepan over low heat, melt butterscotch chips. Remove from heat. Add noodles and peanuts; mix well. Drop by tablespoonfuls onto wax paper; allow to set. Makes 2 dozen.

Build your own hay maze. Stack hay bales, forming a little path that runs through them. The kids will laugh all the way through it!

FUN TREATS FOR
Festive Parties

Butterscotch Nibbles

Vicki Van Donselaar
Cedar, IA

These nibbles are very simple and easy to make! Every year, my mother-in-law and sisters-in-law get together over Thanksgiving weekend to decorate several dozen cut-out cookies and do some candy making for the upcoming Christmas holiday. These are a favorite...they never last long around our house.

12-oz. pkg. butterscotch chips
1 c. creamy peanut butter
8 c. bite-size crispy corn cereal
   squares

1 c. semi-sweet chocolate
   chips

In a large saucepan over low heat, melt butterscotch chips and peanut butter. Add cereal; stir until coated. Add chocolate chips; stir until combined and mixture looks marbled. Spread on a lightly greased 17"x11" jelly-roll pan. Cool 30 minutes. Break into pieces; store in an airtight container. Serves 12.

Caramel Marshmallows

Nancy Lanning
Lancaster, SC

When we were in Iowa for a few years, these were a favorite with all the kids...easy for kids to make too!

40 caramels, unwrapped
1/2 c. sweetened condensed
   milk

1/2 c. butter
50 marshmallows
6 c. crispy rice cereal

Combine caramels, condensed milk and butter in a large saucepan over low heat. Cook and stir until melted. Using a long toothpick, dip each marshmallow in mixture; roll in cereal. Place on wax paper to set. Store in a covered container. Makes about 4 dozen.

Looking for a new no-mess way to decorate Jack-o'-Lanterns? Try duct tape! It comes in lots of fun colors and is super-easy to cut into shapes...great for kids to craft with.

Apple Cake with Warm Sauce

Jennifer Fox
Fredericktown, OH

A cake like this one used to be served at a hometown restaurant.
Every fall, I couldn't wait to enjoy a piece with a hot cup of coffee!

1 c. shortening
2-1/2 c. sugar
2 eggs
3 c. all-purpose flour
2 t. baking soda

1 t. salt
2 t. cinnamon
8 tart apples, peeled, cored
   and diced

In a large bowl, combine shortening with sugar. Beat with an electric mixer on low speed until smooth. Add eggs; beat until well blended. Add flour, baking soda, salt and cinnamon. Beat on medium speed for 2 minutes, until smooth. Fold in apples with a spoon until well mixed. Pour batter into a greased and floured 13"x9" baking pan. Bake at 350 degrees for 45 minutes. Serve slices of cake topped with Warm Sauce. Serves 15.

Warm Sauce:

1-1/2 c. sugar
3 T. all-purpose flour
1-1/2 c. milk

3/4 c. margarine
1 T. vanilla extract

Combine sugar, flour and milk in a saucepan over medium hat. Cook, stirring constantly, until sugar is all dissolved. Add margarine and vanilla; continue stirring until thickened.

A person who can bring the spirit of laughter
into a room is indeed blessed.

–Bennett Cerf

Vermont Maple Cake

Sara LaRouche
Rutland, VT

*Here in Vermont, when the first gallon of maple syrup was
brought home, this was the first thing Mom would make.
There's nothing like our maple syrup!*

1 c. pure maple syrup
1 T. oil
3/4 c. sugar
1 egg, beaten
1-1/2 c. all-purpose flour

2 T. baking powder
3/4 t. salt
1 c. milk
1 c. whipping cream

Pour maple syrup into a buttered 13"x9" baking pan; set aside. In a
large bowl, blend oil, sugar and egg; set aside. In a separate bowl,
combine flour, baking powder and salt. Add flour mixture to oil
mixture; beat well. Stir in milk. Pour batter over maple syrup in pan;
pour cream over top. Bake at 350 degrees for 30 to 35 minutes, until
a toothpick inserted in the center tests done. Makes 12 servings.

A simple harvest decoration for cupcakes! Cut red, yellow and
orange fruit-flavored snack rolls with leaf-shaped mini cookie
cutters, then press the "leaves" onto frosted cupcakes.

Grandma Esther's Cranberry-Nut Pie

Jenny Sarbacker
Madison, WI

Every time I go to the farm to visit Grandma, she always seems to have made some new recipe...well, new to me, but old-hat to her! When I ask, she'll dig out an old recipe clipping, or a recipe rewritten on an index card with countless stains that show its use. She always seems to have a story about the recipe...who it came from, the last time she used it, who liked it and who didn't. Amazing how she can remember all that, with our large family!

Optional: 9-inch pie crust, unbaked
1-1/4 c. fresh or frozen cranberries
1/4 c. walnuts, hickory nuts or pecans, chopped

1/4 c. brown sugar, packed
1 egg, beaten
1/2 c. sugar
1/2 c. all-purpose flour
1/3 c. butter, melted

Arrange pie crust in a 9" pie plate, or simply grease pie plate. Fill pie plate with cranberries. Sprinkle with nuts and brown sugar; set aside. Beat egg in a bowl until thick. Gradually beat in sugar until blended. Stir in flour and melted butter. Blend well; pour over cranberries. Bake at 325 degrees for 45 minutes. Cool before slicing. Makes 6 to 8 servings.

Don't be shy...enter your best cakes and pies in your local county fair. You just may be surprised at how well you do!

FUN TREATS FOR
Festive Parties

Nutty Pumpkin Pie Pudding

*Robin Hill
Rochester, NY*

On a Sunday afternoon in autumn, I like to have this sweet & spicy dessert cooking in the slow cooker. The house smells wonderful, and dessert is ready by the time we've finished our dinner.

15-oz. can pumpkin
5-oz. can evaporated milk
1/3 c. sugar
2 T. pumpkin pie spice, divided
9-oz. pkg. yellow cake mix

1 c. pecans or walnuts, toasted
  and chopped
1/4 c. butter, melted
Garnish: whipped cream

Lightly spray a 4-quart slow cooker with non-stick vegetable spray. In a bowl, stir together pumpkin, evaporated milk, sugar and one tablespoon spice. Spread batter evenly in crock; set aside. In a separate bowl, combine dry cake mix, nuts and remaining spice until crumbly. Sprinkle crumb mixture evenly over batter; drizzle with melted butter. Cover and cook on high setting for 2-1/2 hours. Remove crock from slow cooker, or turn off cooker. Uncover and let cool for 30 minutes. To serve, spoon warm pudding into dessert bowls. Garnish with dollops of whipped cream. Makes 8 servings.

Top off pumpkin desserts with cinnamon-spice whipped cream. In a chilled mixing bowl, beat 2 cups whipping cream, 1 tablespoon orange liqueur or juice and 1/4 teaspoon cinnamon until stiff peaks form.

Mocha Devil's Food Cake

Sherry Page
Akron, OH

When I used to bake cakes for a little extra money, this dark chocolatey cake was a favorite with my customers.

1/2 c. butter, softened
2 c. sugar
2 eggs, separated
2 c. all-purpose flour
1-1/2 c. milk

4 sqs. unsweetened baking
chocolate, melted
1 t. vanilla extract
2 t. baking powder

In a large bowl, blend butter and sugar; beat in egg yolks. Stir in flour and milk alternately. Add melted chocolate and vanilla; mix in baking powder and set aside. With an electric mixer on high speed, beat egg whites until stiff peaks form. Fold egg whites into batter. Divide batter between 2 greased and floured 9" round cake pans. Bake at 375 degrees for about 25 minutes, until a toothpick tests done. Cool; assemble cake with Chocolate Icing. Makes 12 to 15 servings.

Chocolate Icing:

1/2 c. butter, softened
3 to 4 T. cold brewed coffee
1 sq. unsweetened baking
chocolate, melted

16-oz. pkg. powdered sugar

In a large bowl, beat together butter and 3 tablespoons coffee; add melted chocolate. Gradually beat in powdered sugar, adding more coffee as need to make a spreading consistency.

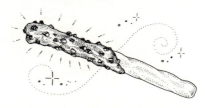

A sweet & salty treat in a jiffy! Simply dip pretzel rods in melted chocolate. Drizzle with white chocolate or candy melts in seasonal colors and roll in candy sprinkles. For party favors, wrap individually in plastic wrap and tie with a bow.

Christy's Chocolate Trifle

Christy Easter
Dover, NH

I make this dessert every year for Thanksgiving. It just isn't Thanksgiving without it! To save time on Turkey Day, you can bake the cake the night before.

18-1/2 oz. pkg. chocolate cake mix
9 3-1/4 oz. refrigerated single-serving chocolate pudding cups, divided
16-oz. container frozen whipped topping, thawed and divided
8-oz. pkg. toffee brickle baking bits, divided

Prepare cake mix according to package instructions; bake in a 13"x9" baking pan. Allow cake to cool completely. Let cool; crumble cake in the pan. In a glass trifle bowl, layer 1/3 of cake crumbs, pudding from 3 pudding cups and 1/3 of whipped topping; sprinkle with 1/3 of toffee bits. Repeat layering twice, ending with toffee bits. Cover and refrigerate until ready to serve. Serves 12.

A garnish of chocolate shavings look so delicate but is really simple to make. Just pull a vegetable peeler across a bar of chocolate and watch it curl!

Sheila's Carrot Pie

Sheila Murray
Tehachapi, CA

Years ago, my sister & her husband rented a cabin for Thanksgiving so the family could all be together. I found this recipe in a newspaper, and thought I would make one carrot pie and one pumpkin pie to see if anyone could tell the different. Everyone loved the carrot one better...they couldn't believe it was carrot!

2-1/2 c. carrots, peeled
   and sliced
1/2 c. sugar
1 egg, beaten
1 t. salt
1/2 t. cinnamon

1/2 t. ginger
1/2 t. nutmeg
1-3/4 c. milk
9-inch pie crust, unbaked
Garnish: whipped cream,
   additional nutmeg

In a saucepan over medium heat, cover carrots with water. Cook until tender. Drain well; transfer carrots to a large bowl. Add remaining ingredients except pie crust and garnish. Beat with an electric mixer on medium speed until well blended and smooth. Pour into pie crust. Bake at 450 degrees for 10 minutes. Reduce oven to 300 degrees; bake for 50 minutes, or until filling is firm. Cool. Serve topped with whipped cream and sprinkled with nutmeg. Makes 6 to 8 servings.

Just-for-me mini desserts are so appealing! Bake fruit cobblers and crisps in individual ramekins...so sweet on a dinner buffet and oh-so easy for guests to serve themselves.

FUN TREATS FOR
Festive Parties

Apple-Topped Cream Pie

Linda Belon
Wintersville, OH

A sweet and creamy apple pie that you're sure to love.

2 c. cold milk
8-oz. pkg. cream cheese,
   softened
2 3.4-oz. pkgs. instant vanilla
   pudding mix

1 t. cinnamon, divided
9-inch graham cracker crust
20-oz. can sliced apples, drained
   and diced
sugar to taste

In a large bowl, gradually beat milk into cream cheese with an
electric mixer on low speed until smooth. Add dry pudding mixes and
1/2 teaspoon cinnamon; beat for one to 2 minutes. Spread in pie crust;
set aside. In a separate bowl, combine apples and remaining cinnamon;
sweeten to taste with sugar. Spoon evenly over pudding mixture.
Cover and chill for 4 hours, or until set. Serves 8.

Peanut Butter Pie

Linda Dayringer
Lenoir City, TN

I fix this luscious pie every year for Thanksgiving and Christmas.

3.9-oz. pkg. instant vanilla
   pudding mix
2 c. milk
1 c. powdered sugar
1 c. creamy peanut butter

9-inch pie crust, baked
3 to 4 c. frozen whipped topping,
   thawed
Optional: caramel or chocolate
   syrup, chopped nuts

In a bowl, beat pudding mix with milk for one to 2 minutes, until
thickened. Add powdered sugar and peanut butter; mix well. Spoon
into cooled pie crust; top with whipped topping. Cover and refrigerate
one hour. At serving time, drizzle with syrup, if desired; sprinkle with
nuts. Serves 6 to 8.

Dress up a pie crust with pretty
scallops. Simply press 2 sizes of
measuring spoons along the pie
crust edge before baking.

Fresh Cranberry-Buttermilk Pound Cake

Pamela Marx
Toms River, NJ

A slice of this cake is perfect with a cup of hot coffee or spiced tea when you're watching the parade on Thanksgiving morning! It can also be served as a dessert with a dollop of whipped cream.

1-1/2 c. butter, softened
2-1/2 c. all-purpose flour
1-1/2 t. baking powder
1/2 t. baking soda
1 t. salt
1-2/3 c. sugar

1 T. orange zest
3 eggs, beaten
1 c. buttermilk
1 c. fresh cranberries, coarsely
    chopped
Garnish: powdered sugar

In a large bowl, beat butter with an electric mixer on low speed until soft and fluffy. Beat in flour, baking powder, baking soda, salt, sugar and orange zest. Add eggs and buttermilk; beat on medium speed until smooth. Stir in cranberries. Pour batter into a greased and floured Bundt® pan. Bake at 350 degrees for 55 to 60 minutes. Cool cake in pan for 5 minutes; turn out of pan onto a cake plate. Cool completely; sift with powdered sugar. This cake freezes very well. Makes 10 to 12 servings.

"Adopt" an older neighbor as a grandparent. Include him or her in the children's ball games and family outings...bake cookies together and share stories over dinner. Your family can help out by weeding flower beds, raking leaves and running errands. It's sure to be rewarding for everybody!

FUN TREATS FOR
Festive Parties

Applesauce Spice Quick Bread

Kathleen Farrell
Rochester, NY

*I've been making this recipe for as long as I can remember
and it's one of the first things I remember baking as a teen.
Truly a family favorite for many years!*

1 c. unsweetened applesauce
1 c. sugar
1/4 c. canola oil
2 eggs
3 T. milk
2 c. all-purpose flour

1 t. baking powder
1 t. baking soda
1/4 t. salt
3/4 t. cinnamon
1/2 t. nutmeg

In a large bowl, combine applesauce, sugar, oil, eggs and milk. Beat
with an electric mixer on medium speed until well combined; set
aside. In a second bowl, stir together remaining ingredients. Add flour
mixture to applesauce mixture; beat until combined. Spray a 9"x5" loaf
pan with non-stick vegetable spray; spread batter into pan. Bake at
350 degrees for 50 to 60 minutes, until a toothpick inserted in center
comes out clean. Cool bread in pan on a rack for 10 minutes. Loosen
sides with a knife and remove from pan. Cool and slice. Makes
one loaf.

Turn your favorite cake or quick bread recipe into cupcakes...
terrific for potlucks and bake sales. Fill greased muffin cups
2/3 full. Bake at the same temperature as in the recipe,
but cut the baking time by 1/3 to 1/2.

St. Louis Gooey Butter Cake

Linda Lesko
Darien, IL

I grew up in St. Louis, Missouri, and this was indeed my favorite dessert. Now living in a different state, I long for this dessert that no local bakery here makes. A good friend found this recipe, and it's as close as it gets. Enjoy!

18-1/2 oz. pkg. butter recipe
    yellow cake mix
4 eggs, divided
1/2 c. butter, softened

8-oz. pkg. cream cheese, room
    temperature
16-oz. pkg. powdered sugar

In a large bowl, combine cake mix, 2 eggs and butter. Beat with an electric mixer on medium speed for 2 minutes, or until well mixed. Pour batter into a well-greased and floured 13"x9" baking pan; set aside. In a separate bowl, beat together cream cheese, remaining eggs and powdered sugar until smooth. Spread over batter. Bake at 350 degrees for 40 to 45 minutes, until top is golden and edges are dark golden. Do not overbake. Makes 10 to 12 servings.

When I was growing up, my mother made all of our bread from scratch. I used to love watching her stir up the bread. She would pour all of the ingredients into a huge metal pan and then mix everything up with her hands. After the bread had risen, my mother would pound it down with her fists. Then after the bread had risen once again, she would make it into loaves and buns. I was always amazed at how fast she could form the buns for baking. I can still smell the bread baking in the oven as if it were in my own kitchen. My favorite part of bread-baking day was having fried bread for supper with homemade warm maple syrup and homemade butter. Mother's favorite part was the heel off the first loaf of hot bread, eaten with honey and butter. She passed away several years ago, but whenever I bake bread and smell that wonderful aroma, I remember her with flour up to her elbows as she made bread for our family.

–Janica Beckler, Lewistown, MT

Lemon Pudding Cake

Ann Brandau
Cheboygan, MI

If you like lemon, you will love this cake. This was one of my mom's favorite recipes. She has been gone for many years now, yet every time I make one of her recipes, it brings back great memories.

18-1/4 oz. pkg. lemon cake mix
3.4-oz. pkg. instant lemon
   pudding mix
3/4 c. oil

1 c. water
4 eggs, beaten
1 t. vanilla extract

Combine dry mixes and remaining ingredients in a large bowl. Beat with an electric mixer on medium speed for 3 minutes. Pour batter into a greased 13"x9" baking pan. Bake at 350 degrees for 35 minutes. Turn oven off; leave cake in oven for an additional 5 minutes. Remove cake from oven; pierce the whole top of cake with a fork. Cool slightly; pour Lemon Glaze over cake. Serves 16 to 20.

Lemon Glaze:

2 c. powdered sugar
1/3 c. lemon juice

2 T. butter, melted

Combine all ingredients; beat until well mixed.

After a big meal, treat everyone to a heavenly light dessert. Spoon juicy fresh strawberries or blueberries into mini Mason jars and dollop with creamy vanilla non-fat yogurt...luscious.

Martha's Sour Cream Cake

Patricia Spagna
Naples, FL

My mother was known as a wonderful cook. Friends would call to ask her to make this cake for them. Of course, she was thrilled to do this for them! This cake needs no icing, because the crust is very crunchy.

6 eggs, separated
3 c. sugar, divided
1 c. butter, softened
3 c. all-purpose flour

1 t. salt
1/4 t. baking soda
2 t. vanilla extract
1 c. sour cream

With an electric mixer on high speed, beat egg whites until stiff peaks form. Beat in 1/2 cup sugar; set aside. In a separate bowl, blend butter, remaining sugar and egg yolks; set aside. In a separate bowl, mix flour, salt and baking soda; add to butter mixture alternately with sour cream. Add vanilla; fold in egg whites. Pour batter into a greased and floured tube pan. Bake at 350 degrees for one hour and 15 minutes. Turn cake out onto a wire rack; cool for one hour. Makes 10 servings.

Hot Mulled Cider

Velda Norris
Slater, MO

Perfect for celebrations in fall and winter.

1 gal. apple cider
2 t. whole cloves
2 t. whole allspice

2 3-inch cinnamon sticks
2/3 c. sugar

In a stockpot over medium-high heat, bring all ingredients to a boil. Reduce heat to medium-low. Cover and simmer for 20 minutes. Remove spices before serving. Makes 25 servings, 1/2 cup each.

If you enjoy hot spiced cider in autumn, fill several small muslin bags with a favorite spice mix. Easy to keep on hand!

Apple-Cranberry Crisp

Annette Ingram
Grand Rapids, MI

Every autumn, my family always visits a local farm, where we can sample fresh cider, the kids can try out the corn maze, and best of all...we bring back bushels of apples! This recipe is a great way to enjoy two of our favorite fall fruits, and it's a snap to put together.

2 lbs. Cortland or Granny Smith
   apples, peeled, cored and
   thinly sliced
3/4 c. fresh cranberries
1/4 c. sugar
2 t. cinnamon
1 t. nutmeg

1/3 c. quick-cooking oats,
   uncooked
1/3 c. all-purpose flour
1/2 c. brown sugar, packed
1/4 c. butter, diced
1/2 c. chopped pecans

In a large bowl, mix together apples, cranberries, sugar and spices. Transfer to a buttered 8"x8" baking pan. In the same bowl, combine oats, flour and brown sugar. With a fork, mix in butter until crumbly. Stir in pecans; sprinkle mixture over top. Bake at 375 degrees for 40 to 50 minutes, until apples are tender and topping is golden. Makes 8 servings.

Fruit pies, crisps and cobblers can be frozen up to 4 months. Cool after baking, then wrap in plastic wrap and aluminum foil before freezing. To serve, thaw overnight in the fridge, then warm in the oven. A terrific way to preserve summer-ripe fruit and a real time-saver for the holidays!

Lorissa's Pumpkin Slice

Lorissa Hiebert
Manitoba, Canada

This is a family favorite at Thanksgiving in our home.
Our kids love it...so do we!

2 c. canned pumpkin
5.1-oz. pkg. instant vanilla
   pudding mix
1 c. milk
1/2 t. ground ginger
1/2 t. nutmeg

1/2 t. cinnamon
12-oz. container frozen whipped
   topping, thawed
3 c. graham cracker crumbs
1/2 c. margarine, melted
Garnish: whipped cream

In a large bowl, combine pumpkin, dry pudding mix, milk and spices.
Mix well until blended. Fold in whipped topping; set aside. In a
separate bowl, mix together graham cracker crumbs and margarine;
press into an ungreased 13"x9" baking pan. Spoon pumpkin mixture
onto crust. Cover and refrigerate overnight. Garnish with whipped
cream at serving time. Makes 12 servings.

Tie on your prettiest Turkey Day apron and invite family &
friends to join you in the kitchen to whip up a favorite dish.
Everyone loves to pitch in, and it's a fun way to catch
up on holiday plans.

Cream of Coconut Cake

Melissa Jones
Crossville, TN

My Granny Enola taught me how to make a coconut cake from scratch. It was delicious, but a lot of work! After I found this great recipe, I've never made one from scratch again.

18-1/2 oz. pkg. white cake mix
15-oz. can cream of coconut
14-oz. can sweetened condensed milk
8-oz. container frozen whipped topping, thawed
7-oz. pkg. sweetened flaked coconut

Prepare cake mix according to package instructions; bake in a 13"x9" baking pan. Poke holes in warm cake with a fork; set aside. In a separate bowl, stir together cream of coconut and condensed milk; pour over hot cake. Cover and refrigerate overnight. Just before serving, spread cake with whipped topping; sprinkle with coconut. Makes 12 servings.

Enjoy an old-fashioned cake walk at your next harvest get-together! Played like musical chairs, each person stands in front of a number placed on the floor. When the music stops, a number is called out. Whoever is standing nearest that number gets to take their pick of the baked goodies.

Caramel Apple Cupcakes

Leah Beyer
Columbus, IN

We love to go to local apple orchards in the fall. My kids love getting fresh caramel apples while we are there. We always bring home more apples than a family of four needs, so when I came a across a recipe for caramel apple cupcakes made completely from scratch, I figured I could make them with a cake mix much easier. The kids loved helping make them and, of course, eating them.

18-1/4 oz. pkg. spice cake mix	2 tart apples, peeled, cored and
3/4 c. water	shredded
1/3 c. oil	1-1/2 c. caramel baking bits
3 eggs, beaten	3 to 4 T. half-and-half

In a large bowl, combine dry cake mix, water, oil and eggs. Beat with an electric mixer on medium speed for 2 minutes. Fold in apples. Spoon batter into 18 paper-lined muffin cups, filling 2/3 full. Bake at 350 degrees for 25 to 30 minutes. Cool. In a heavy saucepan over low heat, melt caramels. Stir in enough half-and-half to make a smooth mixture. Dip tops of cupcakes into melted caramel, or drizzle caramel over cupcakes. Makes 1-1/2 dozen.

Whip up some cake-mix cookies! Beat together a 9-ounce package of devil's food cake mix, one beaten egg, 2 tablespoons water and one tablespoon melted shortening. Add some nuts or chocolate chips, if you like. Drop by teaspoonfuls onto a greased baking sheet and bake at 350 degrees for 10 minutes. Makes 2 dozen.

Shari's Pumpkin Bread

Shari Wilder
Glenpool, OK

I love this recipe because it is easy and turns out right every time.
It tastes even better the next day and is superb refrigerated!

4 eggs, beaten	1/2 t. baking powder
3 c. sugar	2 t. baking soda
1 c. oil	1 t. salt
2/3 c. water	1-1/2 t. cinnamon
2 c. pumpkin pie filling	1 t. pumpkin pie spice
3-1/2 c. all-purpose flour	1/2 t. ground cloves

In a large bowl, whisk together eggs, sugar, oil, water and pumpkin pie filling; set aside. In a separate bowl, mix together remaining ingredients. Add flour mixture to pumpkin mixture a little at a time; stir until well blended. Divide batter between 2 greased 9"x5" loaf pans. Bake at 350 degrees for one hour and 15 minutes, or until a knife inserted in the center comes out clean. Makes 2 loaves.

For a fruity cream cheese spread, combine an 8-ounce package of softened cream cheese with 1/4 cup apricot preserves. Blend until smooth. So delicious on warm slices of quick bread.

Index

Index

Index

Find Gooseberry Patch
wherever you are!

www.gooseberrypatch.com

Call us toll-free at 1·800·854·6673

russet leaves warm spiced cider

spicy pumpkin pie

harvest home

pumpkin patch   Jack-O'-Lanterns

U.S. to Metric Recipe Equivalents

Volume Measurements

1/4 teaspoon	1 mL
1/2 teaspoon	2 mL
1 teaspoon	5 mL
1 tablespoon = 3 teaspoons	15 mL
2 tablespoons = 1 fluid ounce	30 mL
1/4 cup	60 mL
1/3 cup	75 mL
1/2 cup = 4 fluid ounces	125 mL
1 cup = 8 fluid ounces	250 mL
2 cups = 1 pint =16 fluid ounces	500 mL
4 cups = 1 quart	1 L

Weights

1 ounce	30 g
4 ounces	120 g
8 ounces	225 g
16 ounces = 1 pound	450 g

Oven Temperatures

300° F	150° C
325° F	160° C
350° F	180° C
375° F	190° C
400° F	200° C
450° F	230° C

Baking Pan Sizes

Square

8x8x2 inches	2 L = 20x20x5 cm
9x9x2 inches	2.5 L = 23x23x5 cm

Rectangular

13x9x2 inches	3.5 L = 33x23x5 cm

Loaf

9x5x3 inches	2 L = 23x13x7 cm

Round

8x1-1/2 inches	1.2 L = 20x4 cm
9x1-1/2 inches	1.5 L = 23x4 cm